DEFENDING BOYHOOD

How Building Forts, Reading Stories, Playing
Ball, and Praying to God Can Change the World

Anthony Esolen, PhD

TAN Books
Charlotte, North Carolina

Unless otherwise noted, Scripture Quotations are from the Revised Standard Version of the Bible—Second Catholic Edition (Ignatius Edition), copyright © 2006 National Council of the Churches of Christ in the United States of America. Used by permission. All rights reserved.

Scripture quotations marked KJV are from the King James Version.

Excerpts from the English translation of the Catechism of the Catholic Church for use in the United States of America copyright © 1994, United States Catholic Conference, Inc.—Libreria Editrice Vaticana. Used with permission.

Cover image: Baseball home base by Karen Geswein Photography / Shutterstock. Cover design by Caroline K. Green.

Library of Congress Control Number: 2018966063

ISBN: 978-1-5051-1242-9

Published in the United States by
TAN Books
P.O. Box 410487
Charlotte, NC 28241
www.TANBooks.com

Printed in the United States of America

For my father-in-law, Herb, the biggest kid I know

Contents

Foreword

Who would think that a book needs to be written defending boyhood. Alas, given the sorry state of our gelded culture, the need has never been so acute. Our national emasculation is obvious and without precedent in the history of a great country founded by men. Even many a male lamely prattles on about the newest malady supposedly plaguing the *zeitgeist*: "toxic masculinity" (read: masculinity).

Yes, a book defending boyhood is direly needed. And Tony Esolen is just the guy to do it. In a Western world increasingly lacking men with chests, Esolen is a man with courage, unafraid to stand athwart the modernists yelling halt. Esolen himself has been hounded by the wolves of political correctness who have pursued him hungrily. He doesn't care. He's nothing if not fearless.

This book is a counterpunch from what is today the new counter-culture. The likes of Esolen and the people at TAN Books/Saint Benedict Press and, frankly, any serious, traditional Catholic, now represent just that: a counter-culture. They are the sentinels, beckoning us to return to that which is time-tested and true, whether they've thought of themselves that way or not. The mob of radical transformers have sought to remake marriage in their own image, sexuality in their own image, gender in their own image, and even boyhood in their own image.

That is to say, of course, that they desire a boyhood that isn't actually boyhood.

What does it really mean to be a boy? What *should* it mean to be a boy?

My boyhood was over forty years ago when boys were, well, boys. Like Esolen, who opens this book with joyful (but imperfect) memories of his Italian grandmother's house, I constantly harken back to joyful (but imperfect) memories of my Italian grandmother's house (my mother is 100 percent Italian). My kids will attest to that. A million times they've heard me begin, "At my grandma's house . . ." I so often fondly retreat to those days in a tiny house overflowing with kids, grandkids, aunts, uncles, the thriving humanity, the loud voices, the crazy kitchen, the card games and Scrabble games until 4:00 a.m., and, of course, the food. People had their places, their roles, and we all genuinely loved it. Yes, there were shouts, disagreements, blow-ups, but there was laughter, joy, stable marriages.

There was, as Tony Esolen says repeatedly in this book, a "tranquility of order" to it all.

I could go on and on with boyhood memories. Well beyond my grandma's house, my memories of boy-time activities range from the outright wild to the patently stupid. Such is the life of boys.

I remember six or seven of us camping out in the woods with only sleeping bags in what turned out to be the first snowfall of the year. We nearly froze to death. My dad knew, but he let us go. It was part of being a boy and becoming a man. Only after urging from my mom (I later learned) did my dad get in the truck to fetch us.

Turning the heat up considerably, I'll never forget damn near starting a small forest fire outside Brian Fleming's house (we called him "Flem") one summer afternoon as we experimented with igniting various sets of brush in an overgrown lot. That was stupid. I still cringe at the thought of J. T. Zulick and I trying to smash his dad's shotgun shells with a hammer on my back porch before someone mercifully saved us. That was *really* stupid. And we regularly played an infamous type of football game whereby we tossed the ball in the air and obliterated the first sucker who dared to pick it up. (A worse fate awaited the sad sack who didn't do his boy-duty and pick up the ball, which was required of whoever was closest to where it landed.) I would here divulge the commonly known name for this game (universally acknowledged among boys of the era as starting with the word "Smear"), but I don't want the incensed drama-queens of the new thought police goose-stepping to my house to arrest my children for my unforgivable sins of the '70s.

Now I have boys of my own, five of them, one of which, John, I could turn into the next Calvin of "Calvin & Hobbes" legend, if comic strips were my business. The kid provides daily material. Amid a pause in writing this foreword, I heard a crash in the woods. I trekked nervously toward the noise, calling out if everything was alright. "It's okay, daddy," responded John. "We just pushed down a tree."

No one died.

I lured the cabal of boys closer to the house with important news that my youngest, Ben, had just discovered a severed rabbit's foot near the porch. Upon inspection, John enthusiastically proclaimed that the dismembered appendage was actually a "ripped apart and stretched out mutant dead squirrel's head." It was quite an exaggeration, but the other boys all seemed excitedly onboard for that creative prognosis. There were no dissenters.

All of that is part of being a boy, but it's hardly a full picture. Enter Tony Esolen with his own storytelling, and his great common sense. His flashes of memory and strokes of pen are both entertaining and edifying, as is his command of everything from the arts to theology to pop culture. He starts with Augustine and St. Paul and finishes with St. Paul and Caravaggio. In between, in classic Esolen prose and style, he sprinkles in discourses ranging from the young Jesus's relationship with his parents to the grown Jesus's interactions with his apostles, as well as numerous literary allusions and pop-culture references, whether remarking on Tennyson or *The Twilight Zone*, Milton and Shakespeare and Dante, Tiger Woods and C. S. Lewis and George S. Patton, Huckleberry Finn and Horatio Storer, Rudyard Kipling and Carl Sandburg, Michelangelo and Saint Damien of Molokai, Pier Giorgio and Dominic Savio, Laura Ingalls Wilder and Odysseus, or Tom Sawyer or Clifton Webb or Jason McCord. The latter of these characters comes from an old western TV show, *Branded*, starring Chuck Connors, a man's man. There, Esolen invokes Saint Josemaría Escrivá's lesser-known exhortation: *Be a man.*

It is this kind of integration of higher ideas with his wide-ranging knowledge of everything from the best poetry and books of the Western tradition to films and sports that always makes Tony Esolen's writing so engaging. His examination is more philosophical and uplifting than my personal musings of a rube growing up in Western Pennsylvania smashing shotgun shells. And yet he likewise looks back wistfully at vivid stories from his own youth—again, so many of which took me back to my own childhood.

Esolen begins by putting us at ease. He was raised in a structure very familiar to me personally: He and his mom and dad and younger brother and sister (precisely my family arrangement) living in a tiny house (which was big enough) and getting ready for Mass on a Sunday morning. Everyone did that. It was a duty. We all got dressed up and took it seriously, even as I never fully understood it all.

Yet, to reaffirm Esolen's theme, there was a "tranquility of order" to it all. As he would say, things were as they should be, even when far from perfect. But there was a peace and stability that prevailed. It was comforting. We did not have, as we do today, "the restlessness of disorder," as Esolen notes. Today we can't even concede that, gee, there are boys and girls. Heck, a boy can *choose* to be a girl, and vice versa. It's cultural and even spirituality insanity.

Today we flail about in uncharted waters. We live in a world in which reality is turned upside down, or at least a world in which the radical transformers are doing their best to upend it. To their eternal frustration, these ideological engineers are going to learn the hard way that this will not bring them happiness, and certainly not peace (although their misguided, if not malicious, efforts will ruin many lives in the interim). There will not be tranquility amid the disorder that these cultural Jacobins wreak as they wage war on human nature and—to borrow from Jefferson's language in the Declaration—aggressively seek to undermine and redefine the laws of nature and of nature's God.

Thus, this book will frustrate and infuriate the angry feminist at the university, who's sure to stomp off to the "community diversity" czar with book in hand, consigning it to a campus blacklist with a trigger-warning affixed to the cover—all in the name of "tolerance," of course. This book is not for her. Esolen advises:

> If you are a feminist who grits her teeth as she drives in a man-made car fashioned from man-mined metals and powered by man-drilled gasoline on man-paved roads on your way to a man-built college with man-laid brick buildings fitted with man-set pipes and electrical wires as you teach your charges in a partially man-financed Women's Studies class about how rotten men are—then this book is not for you. Read Simone de Beauvoir instead, and weep your tears of *ressentiment*. If you are content to see boys languish in school, because you are more firmly committed to the abstraction of some social equality than

to doing justice to the real human beings in front of you, this book is not for you.

As Esolen laments, that woman's ideal boy is a girl, or at least a boy who doesn't behave like a boy. That's what she thinks she wants amid her insatiable dissatisfaction, as she pulls into a Starbucks fully man-built, from the bricks and cement and drywall to every centimeter of wiring and plumbing, as she sips a grande skim latte that owes its existence to cows not raised in Greenwich Village and not milked by the Women's Studies department at Swarthmore, as she proceeds to her ultimate destination at the Women's March where, on a massive metal platform with speakers built by masculinity and patrolled by policemen with guns, she screams approval as Angela Davis and Ashley Judd and Madonna wail the latest nonsense about abortion and transgenderism.

Esolen knows that this book is not for people like her. Such is also why people like him must write books like this. Increasingly, fewer men, especially in the academy, have the guts to write books like this, lest they offend the nature redefiners. But believe me, there are many men in the university world who would love every minute of this book, even as the militant feminized environment has cowed them into a sissified silence. That is why we need boys-turned-men of courage, men with chests, to speak up against the prevailing *zeitgeist*, against what Pope Benedict XVI called the "anonymous power" of changing moods and current fads and fashions.

So, sit back and enjoy a sobering, sensible, and rollicking discussion and defense of boyhood. And when you're finished, get as many copies of this book as possible to your friends and family. They need it too.

Paul Kengor

Introduction

Peace, said Saint Augustine, is the tranquility of order.

I recall a typical day from my boyhood. It is Sunday. That means we are going to church.

My mother and father will not eat breakfast, because of the discipline that still held at that time, that if you were going to receive Communion, you had to fast from midnight of the night before. Practically it meant that you didn't have breakfast. I wasn't old enough to receive, so I had something to eat, as did my younger sister and my two-year-old brother.

Back then we lived in a four-room house, two downstairs and two upstairs. The three children slept in one room, very small, with a bunk bed on one side and a separate bed on the other. I slept on the top bunk, accessible by a ladder. We all clambered out and managed to get to the bathroom, three children and mother and father. We put on the good Sunday clothes that my mother laid out for us. That meant a dress for my sister and a good shirt and slacks and a coat and tie for me. It was a matter of course. My father too would be wearing a coat and tie, and my mother would wear a dress, and also a light covering for her head, as women then did, following the understanding and instructions of Saint Paul. For the woman's hair is a glory to her, he said, not like the man's, if he still has hair and not a shiny bald pate, and the glory ought to be covered modestly before

1

the Lord. So she did. It was actually formal and attractive, that tradition.

I should mention the shoes. I never paid attention to what shoes my mother or my sister wore. My own shoes were enough to think about. We had bottles of liquid shoe polish in the cupboard underneath the kitchen sink. My shoes, usually black, sometimes brown, would get scuffed, because I wore them to school also—not sneakers. Those weren't allowed. To this day, if I catch the smell of shoe polish, I will be swept back in mind and spirit to those Sundays, and I will be squatting on the kitchen floor again, pressing the bottle and its sponge dispenser to the surface of my shoe, and then buffing them with a brush till they shone evenly. That's what everybody did. Boys who loved football did it, and boys who didn't love football but rather army weapons or hunting or roaming the woods or something else did it; all the boys had shiny shoes. It was a thing to do, to be like your father.

We would then go to Mass, taking always the seats to the right of the center aisle, my father standing at the aisle, then my mother, then the children in order, one two three. I have earlier memories of the Mass in Latin, and then sometimes my mother would give me her missal, and I would gaze upon the words in that mysterious language and puzzle them out, while committing to memory the various parts of the Mass, such as the Gradual, the Secret, and the Fraction, which last word meant something to me long before I heard of such in arithmetic. Other families were the same, and in our Irish and then Italian and Polish coal-mining town, you would see their other whole clans in attendance, with boys and girls I knew from school.

The priests of course were men, and the altar boys were boys, and there were quite a few of them, with their rotating schedule of duties. Otherwise nobody was milling about the sanctuary. We had an organ in the loft behind us, where one of the sisters of the convent, or one of her students, always a girl, would play the hymns. Everybody thought that this was all as it should be. Nor was it the only time in the week when many of the boys and girls would be in that church. We were supposed to enter it when we arrived at the parochial school in the morning, when school was in session; those times would vary, because most of the children walked to school. Then the boys would sit in their pews on the right, by class, and the girls on the left, by class, with the sisters watching and keeping order. When Mass was over, we filed into the school, boys in one line, girls in the other. Many a public school had the same sort of thing in that regard: an entrance for the boys, and an entrance for the girls.

After Sunday Mass, we either went home for a bit—and that was when I got to read the sports section and the comics, and I could shed the necktie and, if it was a warm summer day, the coat—or we went straight to my grandmother's house, to visit Grandma and Grandpa. My mother's parents lived across the street from us, so we saw them almost daily, but my father's parents lived all of three miles away, so we had to drive there, which we then did every Sunday.

My father was one of ten surviving children. He had a sister Teresa, named after the Little Flower, Saint Therese of Lisieux, who died of leukemia on the very day that he was born. My grandmother had a custom photograph of her, in the old artistically painted style, blown up and framed under glass. When I was small, I thought that she was the Little Flower, with her rose colored blouse, her light brown hair with a ribbon in it (there was, I think, some Norman Viking strain in our Italian lineage, making me blond when I was a small boy, though my hair had turned glossy black by the time I was twenty), and her sweet smile. She was a bright child, my grandmother's treasure. Grandma sometimes took out little handwritten school assignments of hers to show what a good girl she was. Of course, since Grandma was a woman and an Italian, she had a large glass hutch with photographs of every one of her children, their spouses, their children in turn, and other relatives whose noses and chins were familiar to me when their names were not.

Grandpa was usually holed up in his room upstairs. He was always kind to the grandchildren, but often not kind to other people, and that was because of something I did not know at the time. He had worked down in the coal mines, as my mother's father had. My mother's father, after fifteen years of that claustrophobic and dangerous work, had suffered a nervous breakdown, and could never hold down a job again, though he did work hard on the plot of land he owned, farming it and keeping chickens. My father's father had to leave the mines when he was injured in an explosion: he fractured his neck and nearly died. So he did work at many a job after that, but he was in constant pain from the injury, and he dulled the pain with drink. There was often a medicinal smell about him, and his chin was usually hard with stubble.

Grandma, ever the motherly sort, would bring out frosted cookies she had made, flavored with vanilla and colored a kind of gold from the egg she mixed in with the dough. She kept them fresh in a big canister from Charles' Chips—Charley Chips as we called them; and in those days the Charley Chips man and his truck would come by every so often, as the Bread Man came from the local bakery, wafting the aroma of fresh bread down the street, and the Coal Man, with the clean astringent smell of the "black diamonds" that he sent down his metal chute into your coal bin in the basement, and the Milk Man from the nearby creamery, leaving bottles of cold milk, even chocolate milk, at your door. We ate the cookies always with Pepsi, which we drank from colored aluminum glasses that were good and cold to the touch, and that beaded up with dew during the summer.

After a while, my father would go to visit his friend, an elderly Italian gentleman who ran what we called a "beer garden." His name was Joe Butera, and I knew him as Joe-Butera, as if it were a single appellation. The Pine Cafe was a cross between an Italian and an American establishment. My father sometimes took me along, if I wanted to go. Sometimes I wanted to play at a nearby playground instead, or, if my favorite baseball team was playing the Phillies, I might catch them on television. Naturally my father would not take my sister to the beer garden. That wasn't because it was a dive. It was clean and fresh, and Joe-Butera was a very nice old fellow. But I was a boy and she was a girl, and it wasn't the thing to do. So there my father would have a bottle of beer or two, while I ate peanuts or red-dyed pistachio nuts and drank soda, and then played around at the electric bowling game, or the shuffleboard table. I remember one of those Sundays very clearly, in the dead of winter, because my uncle from New Jersey happened to be in town with his son, who was about my age. The four of us caught a football game on Joe's television.

My uncle and my cousin were big fans of the team that won: the New York Jets, 16–7, over the Baltimore Colts, in January 1969. I was nine years old, and by then a tremendous fan of the Saint Louis Cardinals baseball team, as were two of my cousins and one of the other boys in the neighborhood. Two years later, as a big present to me, my father went with me, my kid brother, another uncle, his son the Cardinals fan, and Joe-Butera to Shea Stadium on a weekday afternoon, where we watched Steve Carlton and the Cardinals beat the Mets 6–3. My father missed Joe Torre's three-run homer because my brother had pestered him for a hot dog and a drink, and he had gone to fetch them from the concession stand.

I sometimes ask people to do a simple thought experiment: change the sex of everybody in the picture, and see how long you can think about it before the whole scene dissolves into absurdity. Imagine my mother taking old Mrs. Butera, my sister, my aunt and her daughter, to Shea Stadium to watch—it doesn't work. It didn't happen.

We would then go back to Grandma's house after a couple of hours at the Pine Cafe, for supper. What the women were talking about in the meantime, I don't know, and I would never know, even on those days when I stayed in the house. I paid no attention to it. It was their business, not mine. But when supper came, that was my business. Grandma was a great cook, and there was nothing she did better than make spaghetti and meatballs. She cooked the sauce in an enormous cast-iron pot, over a gas range, and to this day, I believe that something of the sharp smell of the gas and the iron got into the sauce and gave it a great pungency, a bite. Whatever it was that she did, the food was tremendous.

If our family were the only ones visiting, we'd sit at the table and she would serve us the macaroni or spaghetti with big meatballs, which you would sprinkle over with grated parmesan cheese. I was a late grower—nine inches in one year, and six inches the next, but by then I was fourteen years old—but when Grandma served the spaghetti and meatballs, I had a full plate, as my father had, and then invariably another full plate, which he also would usually have, and often a third plate. When that happened, everybody would laugh and cheer me on, and my father was proud of me then for being a good healthy eater, though where the food went, nobody could tell. Into boy energy and boy thoughts, evidently.

Whenever any other of my aunts and uncles had come to visit too, I and the other cousins would take our plates to the staircase beside the kitchen, often cousin after cousin all the way up.

The tranquility of order.

My mind returns to those days not because I think they were perfect. They weren't. I was often a lonely child when I was outside of my family, which was, thankfully, very large—thirty-nine first cousins, more than half of whom I saw all the time, because they lived in our town, in the same neighborhood. My father had a high-pressure job selling insurance, and that meant that in my early years he was often not home until late, and by then he was exhausted and sometimes a little impatient. He also had to get used to me in a way, because I was a kind of boy he had no experience of. I was the classic Boy Genius, of whom he was notably proud, but proud and comfortable are two different things.

I should stress the point. When a child is an early reader, that's a comfortable thing, but when a child has a habit of scrawling a series of more than fifty initials, always in the same order and always from memory, that is not comfortable. Many years later I came upon the initials and puzzled out what they were: the first letters of the books of the Bible, in the order to be found in the Douay-Rheims translation. I do not remember any time when I did not know how to read. The Bible was the only book in the house, until my parents bought me a set of World Book and Childcraft encyclopedias, when I was five. I absorbed them. I still remember that the population of Pittsburgh in 1960 was 604,332, and the population of Philadelphia was 2,002,512, and things of that sort. That is not a child whom people would find easy to get a hold on. I thank God that at that time such boys, and some girls too, did not have the strangeness stifled in them by psychotropic drugs.

The Immaculate Heart of Mary Sisters in our school were sometimes ill-tempered (and sometimes sweet), and I see now that it might have come from the terrible crack-up of their whole order that was ongoing at the time. We had between forty-five and fifty-one children in our class, in one room, but the sisters did keep order, and we did learn things, though it was nothing by comparison with what I could have learned had I not been in school at all. Lunch hour was an hour. Some of the boys crossed the nearby bridge and got something to eat at a luncheonette in town. Some kids walked home for lunch and returned to enjoy the last fifteen or twenty minutes of recess; I did that for a while. We were also trooped off to the church every first Friday of the month for confession, followed by the Rosary and Benediction of the Blessed Sacrament.

My brother, far more of the scamp than I ever was, played a game with the other boys in his class. When you went into the confessional booth and shut the door behind you, you would then kneel on the kneeler and wait for the priest to be done with the penitent on the other side. When you knelt, the kneeler engaged a switch that lighted up a small red light over the door on the outside, to let people know that the booth was occupied. So the boys played a game to see who could make the light pop on and off the most times, while presumably one of the sisters wasn't looking. The record was five. And so my brother got the idea of kneeling next to the kneeler, and pushing on it with his hand, and so getting the number up to about thirty. When he came out, one of the sisters was ready with a glare to turn flesh to stone, and she pulled him by the ear up to the monsignor stationed in the sanctuary, to do confession all over again.

Anyway, they were not idyllic times, and we were already beginning to suffer some of the consequences of the sexual revolution all around us. We even had a divorce in the family—one of the sixteen marriages among my aunts and uncles—and my cousin was hurt irreparably by it, as we could see even then. I am not claiming perfection, or even great joy. I am claiming that there was a great measure of peace, of sane and healthy and matter-of-course order, in the relations between the sexes, in the raising of children, and in the acknowledgment that boys were boys and girls were girls, so that even a rather quiet and sensitive boy like me was still in obvious ways thoroughly a boy, and the girl next door who was a perky tomboy was still in obvious ways thoroughly a girl, as she and I both knew very well.

The tranquility of order; and what do we have now, if not war, never-ending conflict, suspicion between the sexes, embitterment, each sex as thoroughly dependent upon the other as ever, yet neither sex willing to acknowledge the gifts of the other? We have the restlessness of disorder. When you have order, you can leave your keys in the car outside and not bother to lock your front door and not worry when your children are roaming the woods; and I mean these things as symbols for a common sense and peace-filled understanding of the sexes generally speaking, an understanding that clears the space for innocent fun, love, and gratitude.

Our confusion has hurt everyone: men, women, girls, and boys. When you talk about corruption among grownups, you must necessarily imply the harm they do to their children, and when you talk about confusions in one sex, you must necessarily imply confusions in the other. The sexes stand and fall together. But it is hardly possible for any single writer to focus on every facet of the trouble. An open sewer laps at your doorpost. If you write then about cholera, the reader should not conclude that you have no feelings for people who suffer dysentery. I will write here about what I know best, and leave to others to write about what they know best. I will write about boys. I do not deny that girls also need help in our time, and that what I say about boys might analogously but also in a different way be said about girls. But I am not writing that book. I am writing this one.

Yet it is fitting to choose boys as the topic, because boys get so little sympathy from anybody, and because, I believe, they have been treated with scandalous shabbiness, contempt, neglect, and hostility, with obvious results in a variety of social pathologies: under-education, under-achievement, under-employment, crime, addiction to pornography, begetting of children out of wedlock, and, in some, a self-loathing flight from manliness itself. Pay special attention to boys, as the brave Christina Hoff Sommers has done in her book *The War on Boys*, and feminists will drum you out of their camp and aim their popguns at you for the rest of your life. Pay special attention to boys, as I am going to do here, and you will invariably be accused of misogyny: a classic case of "projection," whereby people who are eaten up with hate and envy see only hate and envy in everyone else too.

Boys get no love, not even the ordinary attention that you would give to a big and active dog. I seek to remedy that. And I have recommendations to make. They are not mine, not really. They are those that every single person, both male and female, would have made and in other times and places did in fact make, for the raising up of clean, confident, and manly boys. My work is to remind people of reality, and bring them back to something like peace, the tranquility of order—even when that tranquility is to be observed in a heap of sprawling and clambering boys playing King of the Hill, or in all the other things, preparatory to wrestling with the world, that boys once did and would still do if they were given half a chance.

If you do not love those creatures—if you are a feminist who grits her teeth as she drives in a man-made car fashioned from man-mined metals and powered by man-drilled gasoline on man-paved roads on your way to a man-built college with man-laid brick buildings fitted with man-set pipes and electrical wires as you teach your charges in a partially man-financed Women's Studies class about how rotten men are—then this book is not for you. Read Simone de Beauvoir instead, and weep your tears of *ressentiment*. If you are content to see

boys languish in school, because you are more firmly committed to the abstraction of some social equality than to doing justice to the real human beings in front of you, this book is not
for you. If your ideal boy is a girl, or if your heart is delighted
by boys who seize upon the nearest means of drawing attention
to themselves, which is to make themselves pretty and dress up
like girls, in the sad and ghastly fabrications of the "transgen-
der" movement (and I dearly hope that some reader many years
from now, with a shot of whisky handy, will have to look up the
word to find out what it once meant) then this book is not for
you, unless someone should pitch it at your head to knock some
sense into that dull hard place.

But if you do love boys as boys, read on. Men especially—
read on. It is your duty.

The Arena to Enter

When Jesus was twelve years old, writes Saint Luke, his mother, Mary, and his foster-father, Joseph, went up to Jerusalem at the feast of the Passover, as was their custom. After the feast, as they were returning, the boy Jesus stayed behind in Jerusalem. His parents did not know it, but supposing him to be in the company, they went a day's journey, and they sought him among their kinsfolk and acquaintances; and when they did not find him, they returned to Jerusalem, seeking him. After three days, they found him in the temple, sitting among the teachers, listening to them and asking them questions; and all who heard him were amazed at his understanding and his answers. Mary and Joseph were amazed, rather, that he was still in Jerusalem, and Mary said to him, "Son, why have you treated us so? Behold, your father and I have been looking for you anxiously."

But Jesus replied, "How is it that you sought me? Did you not know that I must be in my father's house?" or, more accurately, about the things pertaining to his father, his father's business (Lk 2:42–49).

Let us look at this scene more closely. The first thing I notice here is that it comes as no surprise. I do not mean Jesus' enigmatic reply, but the plain fact that, at twelve years old, he should seek out the company of the masters of his faith, and ask them questions and agree to be grilled by them in turn. Jan

Steen's painting of the scene has the old men of the temple poring over books, searching in them, and disputing among themselves; all of it apparently prompted by the conversation of the
boy Lord. There appear, in fact, to be five conversations going
on simultaneously, while the chief priest, sitting in a niche as if
presiding over the fray, gazes at a book spread open upon his
knees. Steen painted it in 1660, and the architecture is Baroque,
as is his notion of the clothes the figures would be wearing, and
we see distinctly Dutch features in Joseph and Mary. She leans
forward and grasps Jesus gently by the arm, while Joseph stands
behind, hat in hand, his head tilted as he listens quietly. The
boy is looking at Mary sidelong while gesturing outward and
forward, palm splayed out, toward the temple, as if to say, "Here
is where I belong."

The style of architecture does not matter, nor the style of
dress. The essence of the scene is immediately recognizable by
anyone who knows what boys are really like. Would an intelligent and intense twelve-year-old boy seek to distance himself
from the comforts of the domestic, to enter into the masculine world of dispute, of stance and counter-stance, point and
counter-point, to test and be tested? It is *exactly* what such a boy
might do, unless he lived in a world of unnatural confinement
such as ours, with clipped wings and a cage.

Consider another feature. The boy naturally looks toward
certain kinds of *men*, who will grant him the liberty of intellectual and spiritual combat, to dispute and fight about the highest things. It has all the delight of a game, with rules, and the
wonder of a search into mysteries. Its purpose is not to make
anybody comfortable or happy. They are there not to argue
about what kinds of clothing to wear, or whether a certain
neighbor did right or wrong in rebuking the woman drawing
water at the well while the men were watering the sheep. Those
are fine conversations to have, but that is not what draws the

boy to the men. Who knows what Jesus might have been asking? Something perhaps akin to what he asked of the Pharisees
many years later, when he stopped their mouths. He had asked
them who the Messiah was to be, and they replied, "The son of
David." But he said to them, "How is it then that David, inspired
by the Spirit, calls him Lord, saying, 'The Lord said to my Lord,
sit at my right hand, till I put thy enemies under thy feet'? If
David thus calls him Lord, how is he his son?" (Mt 22:43–45).
Bishop to queen's rook five, check.

Or we may recall his encounter with the scribe who asked
him which was the greatest of the commandments, and when he
had replied, the lawyer replied in turn, "You are right, Teacher:
you have truly said that he is one, and there is no other but he;
and to love him with all the heart, and with all the understanding, and with all the strength, and to love one's neighbor as one-
self, is much more than all whole burnt offerings and sacrifices"
(Mk 12:32–33). To which Jesus said, "You are not far from the
kingdom of God" (v. 34).

Combat with rules is a good thing. Steel sharpens steel.
But combat is a means, not an end. We do not sense that Jesus
loved disputations for their own sake. In fact, he was not at all
touched with pride for his skill at the endeavor, and he com-
pared the Pharisees who tangled themselves up in rabbinical
questions, while missing the heart of the commandments of
God, to people who could swallow a camel and strain at a gnat.
The *end* is truth, what really is so: not feelings, not social ease,
not convenience, not a pleasant acceptance of a half-truth here
and a half-truth there. For half a truth added to half a truth does
not equal a whole truth, though it may equal a whole lie—and
often has, in the sad history of man. Not once in the Gospels
does Jesus sigh and shrug and suggest that, to keep the peace,
any portion of the Truth is negotiable.

Boys seek out men because men will allow for the combat, which can be fierce, and often ought to be fierce, but which need not result in hard feelings. Often it results in fast friendships. Men allow for the arena, the space that is safe in *not* being safe. Safety kills.

And there is another thing about the scene. It shows up pretty prominently in Steen's painting. Mary is the only woman there, and with her bright and beautiful robes, Steen has set her as both apart from the men and in a way superior to them. Yet Jesus' reply, which iconographers have always pictured as a reply to Mary, even though he uses the second person plural, suggests that the boy is setting himself apart from the world of women and the home, and establishing his separate identity. "Did you not know I must be about my father's business?" is a question that might be asked by any boy of any protective mother, and it need not be spoken with harshness, but with a gentle and firm determination.

I am not the first to notice it, but it bears repeating. Each of the four parent-child relationships is distinct and beautiful in its way, and each presents its peculiar challenge. In the case of the mother-son, the boy must break away from the woman he loves best in the world, a woman from whom he has derived nurture and protection even as he grows tall and strong and learns to be *her protector,* and in the case of widowhood, *her provider:* such would the young man Jesus be. He must establish his identity as a man among men if he is then to return to the world of women, fit to marry a woman, if such is his calling, and to head a family in his turn. He must be about his father's business. As Jesus was, he was called "the carpenter's son," and tradition has it that he worked at Joseph's trade. Students of the culture at the time say that Joseph the *teknon* was probably what we would call a construction worker, fitting beams and rafters for large building projects in the Greco-Roman cities round-about the Sea of Galilee.

Then Jesus must have learned from his father and from the other men how to deal with that wood: how to plane a beam, how to notch it to be pressed firmly in place, how to tell a good plank from one ready to split along a seam, and, more important yet hard to speak of, precisely because its effect is everywhere, how to work alongside other men. I am not saying that Jesus learned nothing from his mother! He learned from Mary more than we can know. He learned, evidently, the loveliness and the sweetness of women, and how to be gentle with them, as he most notably was—though he was not always exactly gentle with the woman he loved best, his mother, as we will see. That is not the point. I am only saying the obvious: that there were things he could learn only from other men, and that, in addition, they are the sorts of things that a woman will expect in a man if she is to marry him. In this sense, every boy *must be about his father's business,* whether or not he enters it, and must also do the kind of thing that Jesus did when he left the entourage of the home and set himself as a young man among men.

Breaking the Pull

After that scene in the Temple, we hear no more of Joseph, and that has led people to assume that the foster-father of Jesus was considerably older than Mary. It is a natural assumption, but unwarranted by anything we see in the text, and certainly Joseph had to be young enough and strong enough to perform the labor he did for a living, rough on the hands and arms, and heavy on the shoulders and back and legs. He also had to be hale and bold, to take Mary and the small child far away from his native home in Galilee and his ancestral home in Bethlehem, protecting them against the wrath of the Idumaean pretender and tyrant Herod, to go and live in the swarming Egyptian delta of the Nile, among Jews of the diaspora, with nothing to recommend him but the power in his body, the talent in his hands, and the determination in his heart.

Jesus learned the carpenter's trade from Joseph, and so he would have been his mother Mary's sole support after the death of Joseph, but it is hard to suppose that Jesus simply turned on a copper coin at age thirty and left his mother to take up a form of life that she could never have expected. Mary had heard the prophecy of Simeon, that the boy Jesus would grow up to be a sign of contradiction, for the rise and fall of many in Judah, and that a sword would pierce her heart. Her natural inclination would have been *to protect him*, and so we find her, perhaps half willingly, going along with his cousins to bring him back home to Nazareth, because the cousins were worried about him. Perhaps those cousins were worried less for his welfare than for theirs, because Jesus, the sign of contradiction, must have already cost them considerable trouble at home. Yet one of those cousins, James, would be a leader in the early Church, and that would cost him his life.

So Jesus is to Mary at times what he would later be to Peter, when that disciple who was most keenly drawn to him for his wisdom tried to play the manager and took Jesus aside to urge him not to enter the snake pit that was Jerusalem. Jesus would never say to Mary what he said to Peter, "Get thee behind me, Satan!" But he does sometimes keep her motherly care at arm's length. "Your mother and your brethren are outside, asking for you," said the disciples once, when Jesus was crowded round with people listening to him inside a house. We do not know exactly what these cousins at that time thought of Jesus, but it does appear that they wanted to protect him because people were saying that he had gone mad, and the malignant scribes said that he was casting out demons by invoking Beelzebul, the prince of demons. But Jesus replied, "Who are my mother and my brethren?" And he looked round at those who were listening to him, and said, "Here are my mother and my brethren! Whoever does the will of God is my brother, and sister, and mother" (Mk 3:20–35).

But what happens to the boy if he cannot establish himself apart from the strong centripetal pull of the mother's love? What happens to the overprotected boy? Everybody knows what happens. I will now risk inciting anger by saying what the angry themselves know quite well. The boy is spoiled.

Here I will turn, begging the reader's pardon, to the best of our popular culture, that strange series of Christian morality plays, science fiction, and Greek tragedy called *The Twilight Zone*. There's a subtly terrifying episode that, without intending anything controversial then or for any sane human culture, lays its cold steel probe on just this exposed nerve of our time. The episode is called "Young Man's Fancy," after a line from the brooding young man in Tennyson's "Locksley Hall": "In the spring a young man's fancy lightly turns to thoughts of love." Not the young man in Richard Matheson's playlet.

Virginia Walker (played by the wholesome and womanly Phyllis Thaxter) has been waiting for eleven years to marry the man she loves, Alex Walker (Alex Nicol). Eleven years of indecision, eleven years of divided loyalty, eleven years of *falling short of manhood*. The notable event setting Alex free has been the death of his mother, with whom he has lived all his life, after his father abandoned them when he was a small boy. Matheson is canny here. It would be easy to dismiss the mother if she were merely pathological, but the bad situation into which she and the boy were thrust, against her will, brought out her *strength*, not her weakness. Alex says that she was everything to him, and she worked herself to the bone to provide for him, for which he is duly and unshakably grateful. Yet strengths misplaced and misapplied can do as much harm as weakness can.

Alex and Virginia have just returned from the justice of the peace, and are about to sign the contract selling his homestead to a realtor. But Alex begins to pull away from the deal. He begins to reminisce, fondly, with a kind of touching appreciation of a certain kind of woman, about his mother's favorite song—"The Lady in Red." Matheson's audience would have been familiar with the lyrics and the spirit of that song, and perhaps also with its inspiration: the original Lady in Red, the kept woman Ana Cumpanas, who betrayed her lover John Dillinger to the FBI. The Lady in Red

> *is fresh as a daisy when the town is in bed,*
> *dancing and dining and shining with originality.*
> *She's very proper, she's nothing more than a pal,*
> *But oh me! and oh my!*
> *You'd never stop 'er, she'd be a dangerous gal,*
> *If she should meet the right guy.*
> *Oh, the lady in red,*
> *The fellows are crazy for the lady in red!*
> *Is she a study, oh buddy,*
> *What a personality!*

Against *that* woman, what is a lonely boy to do? I will insist upon this point elsewhere, but the sexual power that women possess, their very attractiveness to boys, makes it sometimes necessary for the boy to react *against them* with what will look like scorn, but with what is really a sort of temporary and provisional shield. It is not because boys do not like girls that they keep them out of their tree houses. It is because they like them all too well that they do so, because the presence of the girl, they know, will change everything. They are not sure *why* it will, but it does. More about this to come.

It's not only the favorite song that Alex remembers but also the fudge brownies that Mother made (he calls her by that formal and anthropological descriptor, Mother, and not by what would be more affectionate, such as Mama or Ma), and this and that, and when Virginia grows tired of waiting for him downstairs, she finds him in the attic, like a child who has forgotten what he came there to do. He is not packing a few things as he had promised but rummaging through an old chest, handling toys, things that remind him of Mother, and saying that after all perhaps they should not sell the house. He thinks they should live *there:* which means, practically, that Mother will rule over his wife all the more effectively because she will be unseen, a perpetual term of comparison. And he will be a dependent all over again.

Then, in *Twilight Zone* fashion, an ancient radio turns on, playing "The Lady in Red," and brownies show up, as if the Lady in Red were appealing to her boy from beyond the grave. What a study, oh buddy! Virginia, her patience fraying, breaks out into an impassioned plea. She reminds Alex that he made a solemn promise to her that when Mother died, he would marry her and sell that house. It is clear that she wants to be the mother to *his* children, and not a rival with Mother for the affection of her now grown and aging child. When he bristles, she loses her temper in turn and accuses the mother of having wanted to smother him, to keep him from growing up to be a man. Virginia wants to set him free *from* undue and disordered love *for* the proper exercise of his manhood. She would, I might say, lead him by submitting to him, allowing him to be more than he has ever been.

Alas, it is a false move—though it is not clear that she had a better move to make. At the end of the episode, Alex has disappeared into his bedroom upstairs, and Virginia, coming up the staircase after him, is suddenly confronted from above by the old woman herself (Helen Brown). Mother is strong, domineering, inflexible, confident, and malign. When Virginia cries out that she won't give up, she'll have Alex and he will be a man and not the stunted boy that the mother made him, the old woman shakes her head, with a trace of scorn. "He has made his choice," she says. The bedroom door opens, and an eleven-year-old boy comes out, just a touch over-dressed, as a mama's boy might be, with his hair too neatly groomed, and with a boyish enthusiasm that is not directed toward really boyish things. He is all agog for having fun and ice cream with Mother. The old lady enters the bedroom with him, and the last words are the boy's.

"Go away," he says to the woman who would have been his wife. "We don't need *you* anymore."

I've sometimes wondered if Matheson had in mind the life of the brilliant character actor Clifton Webb. In his case, he and his mother were not abandoned by his father. The woman abandoned the man because he did not share her high-class aspirations and her love for the theater. A mere railroad-ticket puncher, he was. "We never talk about him," she said. She raised "Little Webb" herself, away from men who would be father-like to the boy, and she pushed him into acting when he was but a child; one of his early stage roles was that of Sid, the snooty, finicky, tale-bearing brother in *Tom Sawyer*. Webb went on to specialize in characters that were appealing but like Sid in some way: most famously, in three screwball comedies, as Mr. Belvidere, an eccentric bachelor super-genius. In real life, Clifton Webb was interested in men, not women, or rather only in one woman, his mother, with whom he lived all his life. When she died at the age of ninety-one, he retired into a state of pathological mourning from which he never emerged, dying five years later.

Boys, as George Gilder noted in *Sexual Suicide*, suffer a couple of needs that girls do not. The primary object of love in the home is the mother. A daughter may sometimes compete with her mother for male attention, but for the most part, she takes her cues from her, sharing her interests and the promptings of her sex. Her passage from girlhood to womanhood is marked not by risk, the possibility of utter failure, or the need, in a public way, to secure the approbation of grown women. It is marked by the obvious maturation of her body. It is stamped on her very shape. Women do not subject girls to initiation rites— what would be the point? The daughter's relation to her father is also not fraught with contradiction. Until he is dying, or in very advanced old age, he will *always* be to the daughter as the protector, the shield; he will be stronger than she is, and both he and she will tacitly acknowledge the fact and what it implies. What I am saying here is true regardless of the particular characters involved, their virtues and vices, and whether they live up to the natural roles. We are talking in the first instance about anthropological relations, and only secondarily about the personal.

With boys, there is no such easy passage. There cannot be. The boy, as I have said, must separate himself *from* the object of his dearest love, his mother, in order to establish his identity as a man so that he may marry a woman in his turn, and be a strong man among other men, his brothers. The mother is also a natural object of his latent sexual love, and that makes the separation all the trickier; and we have all met women who are a tad jealous and who enjoy flirting with their sons so as to keep them to themselves. Saying so should not be controversial. Every culture but ours has recognized the anthropological and psychological fact. The last man a woman ought to marry is an Alex Walker, the so-called mama's boy, who cannot be relied upon in a crisis, and who will let his mother dominate over his wife in the household, should those two women be so unfortunate as to live together.

Be a Man!

The boy does not simply grow into manhood, for manhood is a cultural reality built upon a biological foundation, rather than womanhood, a biological reality with cultural expression. The distinction is crucial. Saint Josemaría Escrivá could understandably say to each of his male followers, *Esto vir! Be a man,* and we know what the exhortation implies. Even feminists know, and tremble. It implies that at any moment of a man's life, his manhood is subject to trial, to be won, again and again, to be confirmed or to be canceled. A man can lose forever his right to stand beside other men. He can fall to being *no man at all.*

The old western show *Branded,* starring Chuck Connors, takes that fact for granted. Every episode begins with the scene that sets the logic for the series: Jason McCord is court-martialed, stripped of his insignia, and forced to give up his saber, which is broken in his sight, for having deserted his fellow cavalrymen in a massacre by the Apaches. He is innocent, but knowing that is not enough for him. It cannot be enough, because, again, manhood is a cultural reality, publicly acknowledged. "What do you do when you're branded," sings the baritone in the theme song, "and you know you're a man?" You do as McCord does: you roam as a lone crusader throughout the West, righting wrongs by deeds of courage. You prove yourself and are seen to do so.

So also in the great British movie *The Four Feathers* (1939). We begin the movie with an uncomfortable all-male scene, old soldiers sitting around a big dinner table, telling war stories that are simply terrifying and probably somewhat (but only somewhat) exaggerated, as men may do, while a boy, Harry Faversham, sits there in silence, appalled and discouraged and feeling out of place. That boy grows up in the pattern of his elders and becomes a soldier, because that is the thing to do, but he is not comfortable about it, and on the eve of being sent forth with his three friends into war in Egypt, he resigns his commission, whereupon those three friends and his fiancée to boot send him each a feather, four feathers, symbols of his cowardice and their disappointment in him. What Harry must do then is to win back their esteem on his own: to be a man. He disguises himself as an Arab and goes on to confront the enemy undercover, alone, in situations far more threatening than any that his friends would face, and so by deeds of courage, he earns the right to send the feathers back, one by one.

If this sounds cruel, well, wresting a life from a hard and dangerous world is no picnic with ice cream and cupcakes. Without men like Harry, his father, and his friends, nothing of great consequence in the history of the world has ever been done. It is life-affirming. The woman affirms her womanhood in the life-affirming act of childbirth, which involves its great share of pain and danger, and the near approach of death. The man affirms his manhood not in the mere pleasure of a sexual act but in the life-affirming risk of death, in the cause of something great, something that redounds to the benefit of all.

That explains initiation rites that otherwise might strike us as barbaric: the so-called Sun Dance of the Plains Indians, for example. Boys on the brink of manhood are brought together for a ceremony of blood and pain and endurance. Leather thongs are attached at one end to a pole in the center of the arena, while the other end is attached, by a hook, to the flesh of the boy's chest. The object of the dance is for the boy to pull free, without touching the hook or the thong. It is a bloody and painful and strangely magnificent business. Merely pulling against the thong will not do. You have to strain against it with all your might, and that usually would result in the stretching of the skin so that often, after a couple of hours of "dancing," the stretched flesh might extend the length of the boy's arm, and still the hook would be in place.

What is the point of such a thing? Victory: being acknowledged as a man among men, fit to pursue the buffalo, to hunt and bring back the means of life, and to fight against enemies. The women did not direct the Sun Dance. But they approved it.

Be a man! An analogous command would strike a woman as without meaning. A woman may call another woman a *bad woman,* but her womanhood itself is not in question, not in the public arena to be tested to see if it is real or counterfeit. The woman's body shows itself forth in an obvious way as for the bearing and the tending of children. The man's body is not like that. It is for projection, for action upon the world, action that is made *possible* by his body—the broad and sturdy shoulders, the large muscles, the heavy bones—but that is by no means either implied by the body or a natural and predictable consequence of the body. The woman's body announces, "I am able to bear children." The boy's body, maturing, says, "*I might be able to do a man's work,*" but without the manly virtues, that body means absolutely nothing.

So the boy must become a man. That means that a boy will naturally shy away from girls during his longer period of sexual latency and his also more delayed and more protracted period of puberty. He has the work of man-making to do, though he may be only fitfully conscious of it. It is foolish and insensitive to charge him with hating girls. The truth is just the opposite. He and his friends *like girls,* and are powerfully attracted to them, and that is why they have to keep them to the side for a while, because otherwise the things they *must do* as boys will not get done at all. Boys in the company of girls do not form the strong bonds of male friendship, because they are too busy competing for the attention of the girls, so they do not invent football, map out the forest, tinker with combustion engines, or bring down their first stag. So it appears that for the sake of both married love and the masculine camaraderie that is so dynamic in its cultural possibilities, we ought to pay attention to the boy's needs and strengths and arrange social and educational opportunities accordingly.

This should not be controversial. It is merely what all cultures have always done: all, in every climate, on every continent, from every religious tradition, at every stage of technological development. It is an anthropological universal. Liberals understood it no less than did conservatives, Jews no otherwise than did Christians, people who hung from steel girders two hundred feet above a river as keenly as Indians tracking a herd of buffalo on the vast grassy plains of the West.

The Platoon

Publicly recognized authority comes into play here also. Let us think for a change. I am looking at a jaunty photograph of eleven men building the Brooklyn Bridge. They are sitting on a girder, nine of them lined up one behind the other, facing the photographer, while the last two are standing up *on a girder,* just where it joins with a vertical spine. No man can do such a thing alone. But we need here more than a plurality. We need the *platoon:* we need the men to be one in sweat, stink, toil, intelligence, obedience to directives, authority obeyed and assigned, danger (a single misstep means death), and friendships stronger than steel. Women do not do these things. They never have: their weaker bodies forbid it, and when their prime directive is to take care of small children, because otherwise the race does not survive, what possible benefit do we gain from pretending that women in groups would like to hang from steel filaments over a city, with a thousand possibilities of death in all directions?

Or I see men crammed like sardines into the canisters of an elevator, going not up but down, down hundreds of feet into the depths of the earth, to be stooped at the back all day, hacking with axes at walls of coal, while the "halls" where they work run with cold water, and they breathe the dust and grime all day. No individual man does such a thing. No plurality does such a thing. Only *comrades* do it: only men (and boys, working near the opening, loading the pieces of coal on carts) who are something more than friends and sometimes other than friends. Nor do they leave the mine and go home all thick with the residue. They shower in a vast open place, with no private cubbyholes. They are young and old, skinny and portly, without embarrassment, but with a free and easy matter-of-factness, not sexual and yet profoundly and ordinarily masculine.

Boys too once worked in the coal mines. I am not recommending it—I am noticing it. In his semi-autobiographical novel *How Green Was My Valley*, Richard Llewellyn recalls what it was like to be the youngest boy in a large and happy family of Welsh coal miners. His protagonist, Huw Morgan, has to establish his right to go to the school some miles away by learning to box against the biggest boy there—and he earns the boy's respect. But when Huw graduates from the grammar school and his father, Mr. Morgan, asks him where he wants to go from there, Huw disappoints him and makes him proud at once, saying that he wants to go down into the coal mines to fight alongside him and his brothers, at that hard, bitter, filthy, and comradely work. The boys mainly worked near the entrances of the mines, handling large carts heaped with coal, emptying them and rolling them back to the elevators to be filled again. If you look at photographs of breaker boys, you will see, even through the miserable indignities that the industrial revolution visited upon those children, an obvious camaraderie, darkened with a grave determination or resignation. In this regard to be confined to the coal mines was not as soul-dampening as being confined in a large, anonymous, and boy-neglecting school. At least those boys near the mines became men as they suffered.

But we do not have to think of miseries either. Until people made a pointed effort at making girls more like boys, there is no instance that I can recall of girls or women spontaneously coming together in teams for competitive sports. The *team* is an anthropological constant for the males of our species. Every culture in the world has them, and if we think about defense or the hunt, we can see why. I will have more to say about the structure of the activities that the team engages in, because they reflect or they make evident the structures of masculine thought itself and masculine organization in arts and letters. If I am right about this, then the masculine team may be a necessary feature for the *education* of boys. Without it, many a lad simply will not learn.

Vitamin Deficiency

So we return to the scene in the temple. And I notice that what the boy seeks from other boys and men is mainly public, not private, whereas what he seeks from the girl he likes, or from the woman he would marry, is mainly private, *not public.* Men notably do not talk much about their wives with other men. It is the difference between the arena or the agora on one side and the hearth and home on the other, and their separation from one another protects each of them. This means that, to a marked degree, the boy will be inclined toward what will confirm him publicly and not merely domestically as male, and toward those who have a recognized authority to confer the recognition. He hears the baritone in a way that he does not hear the soprano. He looks upon the broad shoulders in a way that he does not look upon the broad hips. He cannot help doing so.

It is as if there are vitamins that are crucial for his healthy development as a man destined to love women—to be a husband and father; and though his mother can provide some of them, there are others that will be provided by a man, or not at all. What might they be? One of them is to learn how to command and obey. I think here of Rudyard Kipling's boisterous and yet sensitive novel *Captains Courageous*. The boy Harvey Cheyne, a mama's boy, a spoiled rich brat, is swept off the deck of a cruise ship one rough night while he is retching over the side and is picked up by a Portuguese fisherman and taken back to a schooner. His first real lesson in manhood comes when the skipper, a good-hearted American named Disko Troop—who has his own son Dan aboard, a son who admires his father to no end and who warns Harvey that "Dad" knows what he is doing and will not put up with disobedience—knocks him to the deck after one expression of his smart mouth too many. In the ensuing months, for this was back in the day before cell phones, Harvey quite literally "learns the ropes," that is, he learns all that a ship's boy needs to know about sails and rigging, about gutting fish for twenty hours continuously, about how to get along with other men who are similarly under authority, how to fish, how to have a real and masculine friend in Dan and in the Portuguese fisherman, Manuel, who saved him, and how to stand straight and tall, to take severe criticism as you take a dose of pungent and cleansing medicine, to admit a mistake like a man, to shoulder your share of the work without grudging, and to do dangerous and exciting and head-clearing things with other men. His mother could not teach him those things. Not one feminist in the world, from pole to pole and round the equator, will teach him those things, and not least because she would *not* teach him them even if she could, for such things would make him strong, and a strong man's house is secure against thieves, social benefactors, and madness.

They are also a great deal of hearty fun. For it is fun to be a real boy, and a surly and sullen thing to be male and not to have the chance to be one.

The book is called *Captains Courageous* not because Kipling wanted to extol the virtues of men who fished on the Grand Banks off Newfoundland, though he does do that; he met many such sailors during the years when that most poly-cultural and itinerant of novelists lived in New England. The thing is, Harvey's father is himself a captain, a captain of industry, and when the boy is returned to Mr. Cheyne, alive and not dead at sea as he and his wife had supposed, the industrialist meets Mr. Troop—though his wife doesn't want to have anything to do with a mere laborer—and thanks him for returning his boy not as a boy but as a man. There is no sentimentality here; Harvey will not go off to be a fisherman. But he is now determined to do something that would have been unimaginable before he was swept off his spoiled feet from the cruise ship. He will combine the lessons and the skills of both captains and *both fathers*, Mr. Cheyne and Mr. Troop, and go into the business of ship-building and sea trade. His fast friendship with Dan will continue, and be a part of the business too.

Weighing in the Balance

I have spoken about the courage. Now let me speak a little about the captain, not as a person, nor even as a role, but as a brute fact, that there should *be* a captain. Men rank things. They enjoy doing so. It is not a matter of sitting in judgment, like a despot. It is to rate and weigh, to hold at arm's length, to appreciate the goodness of one thing as opposed to the goodness of another. It gives you the delight of being able to tell the difference between fool's gold and the real deal. It too, in many matters anyway, is sheer fun.

If you go to the website of the Internet Movie Database (www.imdb.com), you can check the ratings of each movie, which are composites of many thousands of rankings by many thousands of individual members. A love story like *Gone With the Wind*, very popular among women, will still be ranked by almost twice as many men as women. The war movie *Patton* is ranked by *fourteen times* as many men. The dark movie of social criticism *The Apartment* is ranked by five times as many; perhaps the greatest western ever, *The Man Who Shot Liberty Valance*, eight times as many. The pattern holds good all across the board. The unpleasant feminist hate-fest *Thelma and Louise* still draws more than twice as many male "critics" as female. Top-tier classics such as *Citizen Kane, Grand Hotel, Double Indemnity,* and *I Am a Fugitive From a Chain Gang* typically draw five times as many males as females to engage in the ranking, and this sort of thing holds true across the age groups.

We should not be surprised. Think of the college football rankings. Think of the subtle and intricate ranking systems for placing college basketball teams relative to one another, despite their playing in a wide variety of conferences and against widely varying levels of talent. Think of the discussions that men get into all the time. Who was the greater golfer, Jack Nicklaus or Tiger Woods? (The answer to that question is that Jack was.) Who was the greater poet, John Milton or William Wordsworth? Shakespeare is widely acknowledged to have been the most versatile creator of literary characters in the history of the world. Can anyone stand on the same stage with him? Charles Dickens, I believe, and possibly Homer, Dante, and Tolstoy. Men and boys can enter with gusto into the spirit of such discussions, and end up in satisfying and illuminating and friendship-building disagreement.

What were the most significant battles in the history of the world? Manzikert? Teutoburg Forest? Lechfeld? Hastings?

Waterloo? Normandy? How would you weigh the relative talents of Washington's generals, such as Henry Lee, Benedict Arnold before he turned traitor, and Nathanael Greene? How would you weigh the brutal determination of William Sherman, supposing that it was in a good cause, against the humanity of Robert E. Lee, in a bad cause? What might it mean to say that Emily Dickinson was a great poet in a narrow range, and that Edwin Arlington Robinson was a very good poet in a broader range?

Such discussions spring from a sense of *equity*, not equality; they involve not seeing things as the same, but as different and therefore to be judged fairly against one another. They revel in *inequality*, even as the disputants attempt to set aside all merely partisan favoritism or prejudice. Hannibal invaded Italy. So did George Patton, with his Third Army. Who was the more brilliant tactician? Paul Morphy was the greatest chess player in the world at a time when the theory of chess was still in its infancy. Would he be able to stand up against the greatest in our own time, such as Bobby Fischer? Fischer himself said yes, no question about it. Others grouse and say that Morphy had inferior opponents. But the defenders of the boy genius shoot back that it would not have taken Morphy any time at all to figure out the players of our time. Do you notice how merely bringing up such questions turns our minds toward excellence? And more than that—how, if our hearts are in the right place, we are moved to gratitude?

But surely Jesus was all about equality, right? On the contrary. Envy insists upon equality. Justice speaks the language of equity: of right judgment and balance. Love does more. Equality, says C. S. Lewis, is medicine, not food. We have political equalities because men are bad. I will add to Lewis' wise judgment. If you consume a medicine as if it were food, it will lose even its properties as medicine. It will poison you. We want real food. We want a feast, and only love can provide it.

Remember the scene when Jesus and the disciples are watching people make donations to the Temple. Along comes a poor widow, and she puts in a mere copper coin. Jesus evaluates the donation. He does not say that her gift was just as good as the gifts of the rich people. He says that it was better. They gave from their surplus, he says, but she gave more than that; she gave all she had.

That is a fine example of equity. But love goes farther. Love broaches the mystery of inequality, of a particular gift, of peculiar favor. Jesus chooses twelve men from among his hundreds of disciples and thousands of followers. From those twelve, he chooses only three, Peter, James, and John, to accompany him to the top of the Mount of Transfiguration and to the garden of Gethsemane. From those three, he chooses Peter as the leader of the band: "You are Peter," he says, engaging in the notably masculine activity of tagging a friend with a nickname, "and upon this Rock I will build my Church." That does not mean that Jesus *likes* Peter more than he likes the others. It seems instead that if we judge by natural affection, Jesus liked John better than he liked Peter. But he made Peter the head. He prays especially for Peter, whom Satan will seek to sift like wheat. He prays that Peter will go in turn and strengthen his brothers.

Jesus does not say that all of the saints in heaven will be the same. There will be those who are greater in the kingdom of God and those who will be less. Why should we want it to be otherwise? Would the heavens be more beautiful if all the stars in the sky were of the same middle magnitude, each equidistant from the next, like holes in a grid? I think that boys naturally understand the rightness of the inequality. Better to be the minstrel boy going off to fight in a right cause, girding his father's sword at his side, the least of the army he joins, than to be a do-nothing king, or a mere face in an electoral crowd.

Boys follow the rankings of football teams. Let them rank presidents, then, and poets, composers, scientists, inventors, and statesmen. And themselves; give them a group with the bracing goodness of inequality and equity built into its structure. Let them take delight in the acknowledgment of excellence.

Be Inspired, or Expire

Now then, because your mother cannot teach you the kinds of things that Harvey learned from Disko Troop, and because your mother does not lead you into the world of complex hier-archies, the boy will often be found not listening to women who are "like" his mother. It is not that he is prejudiced against them. It is more accurate to say that they do not speak in his dialect. He may tune them out. He may not hear them clearly enough to bother to tune them out. I attended a Mass recently at which the female lector, with the best intentions, read the readings in a breathy and dramatic voice, as if she were speaking to children in kindergarten. My thoughts turned to football.

Now, if we were talking about any other creature in the world besides a human boy, the solution would be apparent to us and, again, not controversial: "Find someone who can speak in his dialect. Find someone he can hear." I can seize the atten-tion of a room full of boys, in one minute, and hold it for an hour. That has little to do with my capacity as a teacher. I speak the dialect.

We might turn the question inside-out and ask, "What will happen if a boy's teacher is a woman, and she assigns feminist stories for literature, she has a visceral disaffection for rough play, she favors security over risk and equality over freedom and the dynamism of hierarchy; she likes finger-painting more than

football, and for all her egalitarianism, she seems touchy about
any questioning of her authority?" What if it is all *Little Women*,
all the time, but without Louisa May Alcott's very real love for
boys, and her still more than residual Christian faith? Plenty
of tedium, irritation, frustration, confinement, but no hearing.

For the sake of boys and the families they must eventually
lead, we must open our hearts and quit attempting to thrust
upon them an unnatural and uninspiring commitment to sexual indifference. What they need, they need, and the needs are
grounded in ages upon ages of human development both physical and intellectual. They are attested to by every culture known
to man, and by common observation. There is only one word
for those who, for the sake of an ideology, whatever it may be,
would consciously deny to either boys or girls what they need to
be healthy members of their sex. That word is *wicked*.

I do not exaggerate. We are not talking here about grown
men, who have learned how to live with women and work with
them, but about boys—children. It is cruel or stupid or both to
expect from boys a denial of their innate needs, in the service
of some great vague social good that they can neither understand nor enjoy. It is cruel or stupid or both to expect them to
learn how to train themselves to listen to teachers who do not
inspire them, to learn to pretend to enjoy reading books about
smart girls and dumb boys, to learn to duck the head and admit
a lie, that all the evil things done in the world are attributable
to their sex, and that all the cultural and technological accom-
plishments of their sex are but vices, because women had not
been included in the works. Change the persons, and imagine
that it was African Americans you were subjecting to a constant
barrage of contempt or embarrassment, or indigenous peoples,
or Jews. Any teacher who did such a thing would be fired on
the spot. But boys are supposed to endure it, and that itself
is a backhanded tribute to manhood. If any boy were to shed

tears of indignation, he would be laughed at, and his feminist teachers would be leading in the mockery. *He* is supposed, as a mere child, to endure what she as a grown woman would find insupportable.

So it is time for men to take back the education of their sons.

Who else is going to do this job? Who else will find it, deep down, so satisfying a delight as will someone who was himself a boy, and who is still a little craze-headed and wild?

Brothers to Gather

The boy is the father to the man. What kinds of boys, then, do we raise? We cannot answer that question properly without considering *boys in groups*, because that—if we attend to immemorial cultural wisdom across the board and the gregarious nature of the beast—is where boys learn to be boys and then men. It is not "society," whatever that is, that determines them, but they in their boyish nature who, if they are given half a chance, will form their societies. Here Thomas Hughes, in *Tom Brown's School Days* (1857), describes in fictional form what it was like for a small boy to leave "petticoat government" and take his place among other boys:

> Tom, in search of companions, began to cultivate the village boys generally more and more. Squire Brown, be it said, was a true-blue Tory to the backbone, and believed honestly that the powers which be were ordained of God, and that loyalty and steadfast obedience were men's first duties. Whether it were in consequence or in spite of his political creed, I do not mean to give an opinion, though I have one; but certain it is that he held therewith divers social principles not generally supposed to be true blue in color. Foremost of these, and the one which the Squire loved to propound above all others, was the belief that a man is to be valued wholly and solely for that which he is

in himself, for that which stands up in the four fleshly walls of him, apart from clothes, rank, fortune, and all externals whatsoever. Which belief I take to be a wholesome corrective of all political opinions, and, if held sincerely, to make all opinions equally harmless, whether they be blue, red, or green. As a necessary corollary to this belief, Squire Brown held further that it didn't matter a straw whether his son associated with lords' sons or plowmen's sons, provided they were brave and honest. He himself had played football and gone bird-nesting with the farmers whom he met at vestry and the laborers who tilled their fields, and so had his father and grandfather, with their progenitors. So he encouraged Tom in his intimacy with the boys of the village, and forwarded it by all means in his power, and gave them the run of a close for a playground, and provided bats and balls and a football for their sports.

Squire Brown, it appears, is a democrat of the only genuine kind. He believes in the democracy of virtue, which assumes, with Robert Burns, that "a man's a man for a' that," and so he not only permits but encourages his young son Tom to make friends with the sons of plowmen and laborers, "provided they were brave and honest." The Squire, note well, does not assume the role of organizer. He gives the boys "bats and balls and a football," and then lets them go, as they themselves play cricket or rounders or football, intricately structured games that never move one step without an agreed-on set of rules and a hierarchy of decisions. As for the political point, we might transpose the Squire's hearty sense of fellowship into these terms: "A man is to be valued wholly and solely for that which he is in himself," apart from the college he gets into, the work he procures, the political causes he espouses, the money he makes, and the exclusive neighborhood where he plants himself as an intolerant liberal or a heedless conservative. Harvard, go to hell.

Or Harvard, return, Harvard such as you once were, divinity school and mischief making and all. Some boys are huddling in the scar of a bluff along the Mississippi River. They have organized themselves into a society of robbers. Not burglars, because there's no respectability in that, sneaking and breaking into houses and all. No, they're going to be dashing highwaymen. But that means there have to be rules, which the leader of the boys duly invents, in particular the oath of loyalty:

> It swore every boy to stick to the band, and never tell any of the secrets; and if anybody done anything to any boy in the band, whichever boy was ordered to kill that person and his family must do it, and he mustn't eat and he mustn't sleep till he had killed them and hacked a cross in their breasts, which was the sign of the band. And nobody that didn't belong to the band could use that mark, and if he did he must be sued; and if he done it again he must be killed. And if anybody that belonged to the band told the secrets, he must have his throat cut, and then have his carcass burnt up and the ashes scattered all around, and his name blotted off the list with blood and never mentioned again by the gang, but have a curse put on it and be forgot forever.

When someone notices that one of the boys doesn't have any family except for a drunken sot of a father who can never be found, unless he's sleeping with the pigs in the tanyard, they are about to rule him out of the gang, because otherwise things wouldn't be "fair and square," till the boy makes the happy suggestion that they could always kill the old lady he lives with, Miss Watson. "Oh, that'll do," cry the boys, with happy relief.

I hope the reader will forgive me the foray along the great river with Mark Twain in *Huckleberry Finn*. He said, in his preface to *Tom Sawyer*, that most of the boyish shenanigans he was describing really occurred. "One or two were experiences of my own," he says, and "the rest those of boys who were schoolmates of mine." Huck Finn was "drawn from life," while Tom was "a combination of the characteristics of three boys I knew." *Tom Sawyer* and *Huckleberry Finn* appeal to us not only because of the immortal characters—the rascally Duke and Dauphin, the noble Jim—but because we recognize in them the everlasting boy. Even if a boy has never made a blood-oath in a dank hole in a hill by the side of the Mississippi River, he knows that he would have made that oath if he had had the chance. It is exactly the kind of thing he would do.

It is also exactly the kind of thing that made for such places as Harvard. It's clear from both novels that Tom Sawyer and at least a few of his fellows, none of whom is of much use in the schoolroom, have made their way deep into the forests of boyish books, going so far, for example, as role-playing in Sherwood Forest, as Robin Hood and Guy of Gisborne, speaking the primeval modern lingo: "I, indeed!" cries Tom to the wicked Guy, "I am Robin Hood, as thy caitiff carcase soon shall know!" This is the same Tom who chooses which verses from Scripture to commit to memory according to how short they are, and he still cannot manage it. Consider that for a moment, and then ask whether the paradox is ever noticed by the teachers of our boys today.

What I mean is that the boy-society is like the man-society, as Twain intends to show, for better and for worse, but mostly for better. Tom will grow up to be a pillar of his city, as anyone who observed him closely as a boy could have predicted, because he has a keen sense of honor, he turns toward the "rules," and he is a natural head of a hierarchy, a natural leader of men. The word *gang* is a nice English parallel for Latin *comitatus*, the fundamental group of brother warriors that characterized the pagan Germanic tribes; we may then think of Tom as a skinny and freckled Beowulf, and the boys whom he leads in the game, his loyal thanes. It is a lively and soul-making phenomenon to be found in every culture. It is, in fact, the historical foundation of such places as Harvard, bound by the strong bands of brotherhood in a noble venture: *Christo et Ecclesiae* was the college's original motto, *For Christ and the Church,* back when Harvard was a school for men, brothers, to go forth in spiritual battle.

The Gang's All Here

Sometimes things are too near for us to get a clear vision of them as a whole. We almost have to pretend that we came from another universe, knowing nothing about mankind, and therefore nothing about men and women, boys and girls. So we come upon this description of a boy's life in the late 1890s in a small farm town in Illinois: "On the street we played baseball, two-old-cat, choose-up, knocking-up-flies. In shinny any kind of club would do for knocking a tin can or a block of wood toward a goal, though the fellow with a plow handle had the best of it. And duck-on-a-rock had its points—knocking a small rock off a large rock and then running to pick up your own rock to get back to taw without being tagged."

There are quite a few things to notice here. The obvious one is that the boys are outdoors playing, constantly. Girls would certainly be outdoors too, but you could comb the country from one end to the other and not even once find a group of girls playing "shinny," a kind of hockey—with one of the girls wielding the handle of a plow, of all things, for a hockey stick. I am looking at a picture of boys in Ontario, a hundred years ago, organizing a game of shinny by taking a hockey stick and having the two captains grasp it, hand over hand, until one hand covers the top, giving that captain the right to choose first among the other boys. Then the other captain would choose, and so they would go back and forth, thus making sure that the teams would be pretty much of even strength, for the sake of a good game. It cannot be more than twenty degrees out there, to tell from the way they are bound with coats and leggings. Glorious fun, to be playing hockey on a frozen pond in the good fine cold of a Canadian winter.

This sort of thing is not social at all in one way, because the boys do not get together to talk about their thoughts and feelings, but extraordinarily social in another way, because without acknowledged rules and a self-imposed structure, no complicated game can ever be played at all. That they played all day long is attributable not just to their energy but to their creativity and cooperation, making use of whatever they could, and establishing or adjusting the rules to meet the needs of the occasion: the sort of field they had, the objects to throw or strike, the number of boys, the weather, the time they had available, and great delight.

That passage above comes from *Prairie-Town Boy* (1952) by the beloved American poet and historian Carl Sandburg. He goes on to describe activities even more organized than those pick-up games. The boys had seen track and field competitions at two of the local colleges, so they decided to have their own:

> Some boy usually had a two-dollar-and-a-half Waterbury watch and timed us as we ran fifty yards, one hundred yards, a few seconds slower than the college runners, and five or six seconds under the world's record. We knew how near we came to the college records in the standing broad jump, the running broad jump. . . . The mile run we did afternoons, breaking no records except some of our own, yet satisfying ourselves that there is such a thing as "second wind" and if you can get it you can finish your mile.

There's some fine humor in that description. The boys can't all manage the mile, I guess, without some of them getting a stitch in the side and having to bow out. And to be a few seconds slower than the college men at running fifty or a hundred yards is not to be close at all. But the important thing here is not just to notice that the boys ran and jumped a lot. Again it is a highly organized competition, this time with numbers and permanent records. Evidently the boys must have written down their times or committed them to memory. It is absurd, by the way, to suppose that Sandburg and his chums did these things because the adults encouraged them to. Absurd, and untrue. Until our time of constant surveillance and the suppression of children, boys and girls had their own "culture," passing games along through the generations without the instruction of adults. To say that they were what they were because of social pressure gets things exactly backwards. They had the great freedom of life in the open, and such was the society they created out of their own raw wills and instincts and aspirations.

That fits well with another pastime that the young Sandburg enjoyed:

> On many a summer day I played baseball starting at eight in the morning, running home at noon for a quick meal and again with fielding and batting until it was too dark to see the ball. There were times when my head seemed empty of anything but baseball names and figures. I could name the leading teams and the tailenders in the National League and the American Association. I could name the players who led in batting and fielding and the pitchers who had won the most games. And I had my opinions about who was better than anybody else in the national game.

Again, let us try to imagine that we know nothing of this species, *Homo sapiens*. What Sandburg describes here is not out of the ordinary for American boys. What does it reveal or

suggest about them? Organization, for one thing; a penchant
for numbers; the relish of competition, with many objective
standards of excellence; and a natural tendency to *rank things,*
as I have noted before, arranging them in an order and coming
up with reasons for the ranking. We can easily imagine Carl getting into a heated debate with his kid brother Martin over the
relative merits of Amos Rusie and Addie Joss, each boy bringing
forth numbers as witnesses. In fact, I myself have done precisely
that, a few days ago with my brother, as we were arguing about
who belonged in the baseball Hall of Fame and who didn't. The
glove-wizard Bill Mazeroski at second base did not fare well in
our discussion, but a couple of guys almost as good with the
glove and much better with the bat did.

Forget for the moment that we are talking about the sexes.
Merely suppose that the actions Sandburg describes are those
of a species that you the space-traveler have discovered. What
kind of *schools* would the members of that species establish?

We could make a fair guess. They would involve hierar-
chies, clearly established rules, ranks in excellence, and a kind
of combat. They would be the scholarly analogue of baseball
or football or shinny and whatnot. Those boys who, because of
some neurological peculiarity, or poor eyesight, or an aversion
to blood and filth, would not find football appealing, might
very well find that *other kind of combat* appealing. Some football players play football, while other football players hate football and play chess instead.

We would expect not the "safe space," where feelings are val-
idated, but the unsafe space, the space cordoned off for danger,
like the "squared circle" of the boxing ring, where feelings are
neither here nor there, but excellence is what counts, excellence
in the pursuit of what works, what is grand or beautiful, and
what is true. And of course that is the kind of school that boys
do make, when they are left to themselves to make it. Again we

can go from the sublime to the silly and back to the sublime again. We may think of the bachelors of old, rolling up their sleeves, ready to answer questions on the spot, in the public squares of medieval Paris, in sight of all and any—a fierce and friendly combat between the masters and the student, eager to prove his worth in the arena.

I have read recently that full 61 percent of college women now say that freedom of speech does not protect what will hurt someone's feelings. I am ashamed to note that the same survey says that a third of men agree with the women in that regard, or say they do. "Brood of vipers," Jesus called the Pharisees, but now he would be sent up to the Human Resources department to face a coldly smiling Ms. Caiaphas, who would advise the poor benighted fellow that such talk is not helpful for building up "community," whatever that is, or for protecting the rights of downtrodden scribes. Something, anything, rather than the free exercise of moral and intellectual muscle. Higher education thus comes to an antisocial end; deadened by niceness, it is transformed into a place where nobody ever goes on the offense, but rather everyone is made to know, by subtle bureaucratic pressure and social etiquette, what is To Be Believed by All Right-Thinking People. It is the worst of grade school, made mandatory right through the doctorate. Men have not created such places for themselves: that is an historical fact.

Nor have they made such places for the raising of boys. Here we can return to the school fondly remembered by James Hilton in *Goodbye, Mr. Chips*; where Mr. Chipping, having acquired the faintly insulting and yet also amiable name of "Chips" from year after year of grubby, ignorant, mischievous, work-shirking, bright, inventive, healthy, intelligent, and loyal boys, can win their hearts with an insult that spans the generations. "Colley," says Chips to a new lad at Brookfield, punctuating his remarks with a deadpan clearing of his throat, "you

are—umph—a splendid example of—umph—inherited traditions. I remember your grandfather—he could never grasp
the Ablative Absolute. A stupid fellow, your grandfather. And
your father, too—umph—I remember him—he used to sit at
that far desk by the wall—he wasn't much better, either. But I
do believe—my dear Colley—that you are—umph—the biggest
fool of the lot!" And the boys roar with laughter. It is Mr. Chips'
way of welcoming Colley.

It is the same Chips, brought out of retirement during
the first World War, who delivers these words to the boys in
his Latin class, when the sounds of war roundabout them
tend to distract their attention: "It may possibly seem to you,
Robertson—at this particular moment in the world's history—
umph—that the affairs of Caesar in Gaul some two thousand
years ago—are—umph—of somewhat secondary importance—
and that—umph—the irregular conjugation of the verb *tollo*
is—umph—even less important still. But believe me—umph—
my dear Robertson—that is not really the case."

Just then, says Hilton, there was a really loud explosion
nearby. But Chips maintains his composure, assures the boys
that things that have mattered for two thousand years are not
going to change just because of some "Stink Merchant," and
calls on a boy to read a particular passage on a certain page.
The boy does, in Latin, and wonder of wonders, it applies to the
current unpleasantness. "This was the kind of fight in which
the Germans busied themselves," the boy puzzles it out, and the
boys all laugh with the recognition of a good jest, a jest against
the bombers from above (a "vulgar" way of killing people, Chips
will say), and a confirmation of the rightness of what they are
doing in school, despite all appearances.

The right risks bring health and strength. Safety kills.

The City, not the Hearth

Since the nineteenth century, it has been taken for granted in English-speaking countries that women "civilize" men, but I think we had better watch our steps. The word *civilization* there has to do with a perceived contrast between the way good gentle Anglophone people lived in their towns and the way the natives in North America or Africa lived out on the plains or in the forests. That is, the relations between the sexes were taken as corresponding to the relations between races, white and other. Jefferson noted that American Indian men made their wives carry water and do the bulk of heavy labor outside of hunting and making war, while the white men in their families spared their women most of that labor, doing much of it themselves. That was why, he said, the Indian women were stronger than white women, but white men were stronger than Indian men.

I have no idea whether what Jefferson said was true. I rather doubt it. Perhaps Jefferson never inquired too closely into the kinds of work that ordinary farm women did every day. But the point is that men came to be seen as rough-edged and brutish, requiring the civilizing touch of the woman, just as the Indian required the civilizing touch of the white man. That went along with the Industrial Revolution, which stole the man out of his home or from his ancestral farm and pitched him into a brutal, spiritually unproductive, and socially destructive wage-competition against other men. As wise a teacher of boys as Louisa May Alcott's heroine Jo March was, she and her gentle husband Professor Bhaer thought it was needful to teach boys alongside of girls so that the girls would impart to them some of their gentleness and sweetness of temper. Much of the first wave of feminism in the nineteenth century had that cast, not of hatred of men—though there was that too, as Dickens satirized it in the person of the household detesting and generally impenetrable Miss Wisk in *Bleak House*—but of pity for them. They were the Beasts who needed to be tamed by Beauty.

All that sounds plausible enough to our ears, yet I do not see that notion anywhere else in literature. I do not find it in the ancient world. The sea-goddess Tiamat, in the Babylonian *Enuma Elish*, is an embodiment of chaos and passion, and must be destroyed by a coalition of gods led by Marduk, with her dismembered limbs providing the raw stuff for the creation of the physical world. Her consort Kingu is also slain, and mankind is formed out of his blood. The Greek earth-mother Gaia, spontaneously procreative, is a benign goddess, yet in general the goddesses of the earth or the region under the earth are powerful and dangerous: the Furies. The *Oresteia* by Aeschylus may be read as an epic drama about the very possibility of a civilization, and that possibility requires the subordination of the Furies to reason and to the adjudication of men meeting together to ascertain what is right. Blood vengeance is associated not with the man but with the woman, Clytemnestra the queen, mourning the death of her daughter Iphigenia and plotting—like a man in her strategy—for ten years to destroy her own husband, who slew Iphigenia in a sacrifice demanded by the goddess Artemis.

If we turn to Rome, we see Virgil, deeply suspicious of sexual passion, embody in the goddesses Juno and Venus the two great disruptive forces in human existence, forces that can ruin lives and cities and empires: *furor* and *amor*, rage and love. We find Juno still nursing a hatred of the Trojans because of that time when the shepherd boy Paris took Venus' bribe rather than hers or Minerva's (to use the Roman names for Hera, Aphrodite, and Athena), preferring the most beautiful woman in the world to power or wisdom. Paris awarded the golden apple to Venus, who awarded Helen to Paris, though Helen was already married; hence the Trojan War, that undid the knees of many thousands of men, both Greek and Trojan. We find Venus employing trickery to have the Carthaginian queen Dido fall madly in love with Aeneas just so that Aeneas and his men will find a welcoming harbor in Carthage. The result of that liaison, which must be severed when Aeneas is ordered to proceed along his fated journey to Italy, will be rage and suicidal madness for Dido. With her dying breath, she curses the future state of Rome and summons up a great avenger, who will be all for war, never-ending war between the Romans and the men of Carthage. That avenger will be named Hannibal, as all of Virgil's readers knew. How many thousands of men died in the three Punic Wars, I do not know. I do know that more than twenty thousand Romans died in one day at the battle of Lake Trasimene, and more than thirty thousand in one day at Cannae.

My point is not to say that women are as those old poets said. It is to cast into doubt the meaning of the word *civilization* when we look at the influence of women upon men. I call it rather "domestication," and this is well attested. When a man marries, the ancients observed, he will be naturally the less ready to fight for his nation. He will place his family first. The woman has an altogether salutary influence upon the man's manners. But manners in a home and a neighborhood are not laws in a city. Laws and manners make up the weave of a society. Each is necessary, and each is related to the other, but they are not the same.

It is men who civilize men: who build the city and establish its laws. That is just an anthropological and historical fact. It appears to have been recognized by the progressive reformer William Reuben George, who tried at first to help troubled youth by getting them out of the swarming cities, ridden with diseases physical and moral, and out into the fresh air. That was good as far as it went, but George determined that it did not go far enough. So he established the first George Junior Republic:

a place where boys and young men could go and work off their criminal sentences by learning trades, playing sports, and *governing themselves*. I am looking at an early photograph of about two hundred such boys, almost all of them wearing a coat and tie, from about ten years old to eighteen, standing or sitting and evidently looking sidelong in the direction of a master of ceremonies or someone. Some of them have arms slung around their neighbor's shoulder. The smaller boys are seated up front, cross-legged. Many of them are smiling at whatever it was that was being said or done off camera. They have been formed into a real republic. It must be so, since two hundred boys and young men could clearly raze to the ground any building or village if they so chose and if no one shot them to put a stop to it. They have learned to enact and enforce and follow the laws—*their* laws. Would they have done so in the company of girls? I shudder to think what those little ruffians would have done.

Come, Follow Me

Let us again consider the actions of the Lord, who singled out twelve men from among his disciples to form a tight-knit band. I've heard people say that he did so because he was conceding a point to the culture roundabout him. He chose only men for apostles because that is what people would have expected him to do. That explanation does not seem plausible to me. First, Jesus is not known to concede anything to anyone, and that is why they nailed him to the cross. Second, that would empty the apostolic band of all real theological significance, since Jesus' choice of *those men* would have been, in part, without a proper cause. It would be as if Jesus had decided, let's say, to choose Peter because Peter happened to be a kinsman of the chief priest by marriage, and Jesus wanted to try to anticipate any criticism from that quarter. In no case do we ever see Jesus as the politician. Had he been one of those, I suspect that the temptation in the desert, when Satan spread before him all the kingdoms of the world, would have had a very different outcome. Perhaps in some other universe a politician at heart has been known to refuse the offer of power. I have yet to encounter it.

But the main reason why that dismissive explanation is not plausible to me is that it sets aside the very real humanity of the Lord. Jesus was both man and God, and as man he was also *a man,* that is, a man in the specific sexual sense. He had a man's shoulders and back, a man's appetite, a man's rough hands—with the extra layer of skin, useful when you are doing things like planing a beam. He had a man's voice, and a man's musculature. In his humanity, he too needed friends, and in the case of the apostles, he established a veritable band of friends, a band of brothers.

Why should this strike us as strange? Jesus learned the trade of carpentry from Joseph. We think of it as a matter of course. Jesus loved his mother, and treated women with gentleness or playfulness, even a serious playfulness, as he coaxed the Samaritan woman at the well into admitting her sins. That is a matter of course. He was notably *not gentle* with his own sex, when men did bad things; think of the whip of cords he tied together to overturn the tables of the merchants in the Temple. He gave his disciples and even his closest male friends many a verbal cuff, and some of them must have stung. "Get thee behind me, Satan!" he says to Peter. That too is a matter of course. Then why should we be surprised that he selected men to be his brothers in arms? For strategy? No more than that? That would be much, but there must be more. We may now recall the solemnity of the final meal he shared with them before his death, a meal that he filled with new symbolic actions, as if he were establishing for all time—as indeed he did—the rules of the "game" of prayer and worship; and during that meal, he

makes a point of calling these men not his servants or his disciples but his *friends*.

Again I say that there is no need to justify so human and so
natural a social group. It is not that boys were somehow magi-
cally "socialized" into doing the same kinds of things in a thousand different places and times, independent of one another.
If you flip a coin a thousand times and come up heads each
time, I believe it is a safe guess to suppose that the coin has two
heads, and coming up heads is what the coin is going to do.
On the contrary, boys in our particular and very peculiar time
have been forcibly socialized or institutionalized *out of and
away from* such groups, just as both boys and girls have been
forcibly socialized or institutionalized *out of and away from*
regular encounters with nature itself. But even if those groups
were not a direct expression of boyish nature, as they are, their
astonishing dynamism is far more than sufficient justification
for their existence. We are talking about the kind of group that,
arising out of the gymnasia of ancient Greece, invented democracy, devised whole systems of philosophy, hit upon that rare
literary bird called the drama, and produced one of the two or
three greatest periods of cultural flourishing the world has ever
known. We are talking about the kind of group that, under the
rule of Saint Benedict, turned the forests and swamps of northern and central Europe into arable land, and the land into cen-
ters of economic and intellectual light. It is the kind of group
that, in the studios of the Renaissance masters, gave the world a
burst of art that is unparalleled for breadth and depth of genius
so that every small village in Italy boasted one or two painters
or sculptors who, if they were alive today, would be renowned
across the world.

Some people may say that if we leave the boys to themselves, or let them be led by men who were once boys and who
speak the boyish language, we would be raising young men who

cannot be comfortable with women in the workplace. They will be "toxic," say the bigots. I suspect that the real reason that objection is brought up, though, is *not* that people fear that the boys will be poor workers. It is that they fear their excellence: the boys will be too confident, too productive, too assertive, too creative. They will be impossible to dominate.

Let that be as it may. If the choice is between Michelangelo and equality, I will take Michelangelo, and gladly, because his excellence is a gift to all human beings, men and women both.

An Unfortunately Necessary Addendum

As I write these words, the Catholic Church in the United States and elsewhere has been rocked by another earthquake of scandal involving priests and prelates and the teenage boys and young seminarians they preyed upon. Since I have spoken in praise of the creative power of the male group in ancient Greece, I feel I must meet the obvious objection, that those Greek men were not altogether admirable in their ways toward boys, as they made them the frank objects of homosexual desire.

Not all Greek men approved of it, as we can gather by reading between the lines of Plato's *Phaedrus* and *Symposium;* it appears that some fathers tried to protect their sons from unwanted attention from other men. The elder Plato grew more severe in this matter as in others, and cast a sour look upon it for its unnatural character. In Greece, the practice was considered as distinct from effeminacy, which the Greeks despised, just as they ridiculed grown men who did sexual things with grown men. And now, of course, the feminists among us, who understand as much about what it is like to be a boy as I understand about what it is like to nurse a child at the breast, say that the relations between Greek men and the boys they debauched were all about power, nothing but power. Strange that such an idea seems never to have entered the heads of the poets and soldiers among those Greeks, or the heads of such detached and deliberate evaluators of good and evil as Thucydides and Plutarch.

I think that the cause of this sexual desire in such men is almost too near to notice. It has nothing to do with power and everything to do with the natural beauty of the creature in question. It is embarrassing to use the word *beauty* when you are talking about boys, who rightly blush to hear it and might want to throw a punch at someone who accused them of it. But if we are going to protect our sons in this perfectly insane time, we should face the facts, and not be diverted from them by political sentimentalities. Men who want to do sexual things with other men—that is, with male bodies—will look upon the boy's body with a desire that ordinary men will find baffling at best and profoundly uncomfortable to consider. The boy's body is youthful and girlish without being the body of a girl. It will still be soft and not rough. It will suggest the musculature of the grown man, but with the feminine gentleness that men *by nature and not by perversion* seek to cherish and protect. The average sixteen-year-old girl looks much more like a woman than the average boy of the same age looks like a man. Hence there are going to be homosexual men attracted to *that* set of features in the boy. A lot of them, too.

Shame used to be sufficient in most Christian countries and in most circumstances to keep the sodomites at bay. Shame works no longer. Boys must be protected from those who would corrupt their incipient manhood by enticing them into perversions, and good-looking boys, in our time, will be especially vulnerable to lurid suggestions, assault, and seduction. Shame on the Boy Scouts for forgetting that boys are boys who must be led into healthy manhood and not asexual persons to be set up as attractions for the vitiated. Shame on the Church for forgetting it too—and for everyone else who waves the flag that sends the clear message to ordinary boys struggling to become men that their natural needs must come last, and the unnatural desires of men who have failed in the quest for full sexual maturity—such maturity as would make them attractive and attracted to women, and ready to become stable husbands and fathers—must come first.

Look to it, fathers of sons. Let them know what is going to happen. Teach them the value of the cross—the *right cross*, for self-defense and a speedy end to the proposition. Christ, who overturned the tables of the moneychangers, and who would hang a millstone round the neck of a corrupter of children, would not disapprove. Train up their indignation and their sense of what real men do and do not do. Nobody else will.

Mountains to Climb

After Jesus was baptized by John, the evangelists tell us that he went into the wilderness where he fasted for forty days, and was tempted by Satan. "He was with the wild beasts," says Saint Mark, "and the angels ministered to him" (Mk 1:13).

I like that enigmatic detail, "he was with the wild beasts." I can well imagine Jesus reminiscing about it before the apostles, and then the one among them who would best remember it, Peter the fisherman, who also spent much of his time around wild things, would go on to relate it in turn to his disciple Mark.

The wild beasts. Jesus must have seen them often enough. It is hardly credible that only at the age of thirty did he begin to retreat into the mountains and the wilderness to pray. All through the Gospels, we see him involved in the world of nature, often alone, sometimes with but a few of the disciples, such as the three chosen apostles who climbed to the top of Mount Tabor with him, where "he was transfigured before them, and his garments became glistening, intensely white, as no fuller on earth could bleach them" (Mk 9:2–3). That comment sounds like an eye-witness' memory of a past thought, and it probably came from Peter, who went on to suggest to Jesus that they make the place a "home": "Let us make three booths," he said, one for Jesus, and one each for the two great prophets who had appeared with him, Moses and Elijah (v. 5).

"For he did not know what to say," says the evangelist, recording still another memory of an interior feeling (v. 6). But the feeling that animated Saint Peter should warm the heart of every boy. It is made up of the sheer joy of being in a strange and wild place, among wonders, even those that bring fear, and of *taming* that place, building a shack there; camping out with Jesus and his fellows James and John on the top of a mountain, a place otherwise uninhabited except for the beasts with their fearful and glaring eyes.

Then we have that fine moment upon the Sea of Galilee, a large lake prone to violent storms. Some of the apostles are in the boat when the wind and the waves begin to surge, and it looks as if they will never see the shore again. For "the waves beat into the boat, so that the boat was already filling," but Jesus was "in the stern, asleep on the cushion" (Mk 4:37–38), more of those details that can best be explained as the happenstance memories of someone who was there, as one person will remember this and another that. But notice that apparently Jesus was comfortable enough in a badly rocking boat to be fast asleep. He is used to such things. The words of Shakespeare's sleepless King Henry IV, addressed to Sleep, are apropos:

> *Wilt thou upon the high and giddy mast*
> *Seal up the ship-boy's eyes, and rock his brains*
> *In cradle of the rude imperious surge*
> *And in the visitation of the winds?*

When Jesus awakes, because the apostles say they are going to die, he commands the elements to be still, and turns to his comrades, with a trace of impatience in his voice, saying, "Why are you afraid? Have you no faith?" (Mk 4:38–40). Jesus, the landsman, might as well have been the boy in the crow's nest of a ship swaying back and forth in rough seas, rocked to sleep by the motion.

When it comes to raising boys these days, we are lax where we ought to be firm, and rigid where we ought to be free. Encounter with the natural world is not supposed to begin with the age of majority. If by age eighteen you have never known what it is like to roam about the woods for the sake of it, to find things to eat, to explore paths that might peter out or go on for miles, or just to think in peace, you probably never will know it. You will certainly not know it with the same second nature that would be yours if that natural world had grown into you in your childhood and youth so that you know more things about it than you can number or name or put into words. It is a form of child abuse to make it nearly impossible for a child to take the chances of the wilds. Children were not meant to thrive in padded cells—especially not padded cells supplied with moral poison and quicksand and madness. We protect them from wild persimmon, but not from pornography. We protect them from the cry of a red-tailed hawk, but not from the chatter of antisocial media. Their bare toes will not know the grip of a good beech tree to climb, but their fingers will know what button to click to lose themselves in unreality. Their faces will not be ruddy as young David's was. If you look at a photograph of a twelve year old boy in 1900, you will see the face and neck of someone who obviously has spent all of his spare waking hours outdoors, doing things. Our children are pallid and thin, or pallid and pudgy, but pallid all the same, of both body and soul.

That hurts all children, but it must necessarily be worse for the sex that needs more acreage, so to speak: the sex that is made for the hunt, the voyage, the climb, the risk. We know this already. We know that far more boys than girls will find intolerable the confinement of modernity, to which they are subjected all day long in school. Their revulsion from that non-life is sometimes so strong we have had to diagnose them with disorders, when in fact those boys *are in order,* and the unnatural circumstances to which their spirits are subjugated are *in disorder*. A big and active dog frets himself to death in a cage, no matter how comfortable you make it, and not all the pictures of cats and squirrels will comfort him. We do not do to dogs what we do to boys. Many a man-child by his perfectly intelligent and active nature is not meant for confinement even if it is made somewhat mild and pleasant. His eyes turn to the window. His mind turns to other things, especially if what he is fed in the schools is low-fat feminism, with the flavor of cardboard. There is nothing wrong with such a boy. People used to know this about boys and would give their bodies and souls the freedom, the vigorous action, the work and the play they need. That was not when people were saints; people have never, in great numbers, been saints. It was when people were sane.

Here, for example, is an account of what a boy named Stubby saw when first he was brought within sight of Boys Town in Nebraska: "At the foot of the hill, in plain view of his eyes, was a ball field—full of boys screaming like wild Indians. And all around were broad, verdant fields still green with vegetation and trees. And great buildings and schoolhouses, and cottages with red roofs, blue roofs—and a church with a tower and swinging bell that now began to peal out the sunset hour" (From *Father Flanagan of Boys Town*).

There was, say the authors, Fulton Ousler and Will Ousler, no gate, "no fences, no outer doors, no bars, and no locks." Man had not yet known our anti-culture of confinement and constant surveillance. There were no policemen with tasers or revolvers. There were no metal detectors. And that was for a "town" alive with hundreds and hundreds of boys, some of whom had committed serious crimes. But the judges in those days had come to see that Boys Town with its freedom and its freedom-making moral laws was far better for boys than prison was, so they were happy to take a gamble with it, a gamble that almost always paid off, in boys who became energetic and productive men.

I understand that there are people who, if they see a child roaming the neighborhood alone or even with a brother or sister, will report it to the police. That is evil. It means, practically, that they would trammel the children up and compel them to wander a wilderness more dangerous and vicious by far than anything in the jungles of the Amazon—the internet, that is. Such people generally are all right with passing before the eyes of those same children the morbid sexual practices and inclinations of our time. Hunting for tadpoles? Call up the humanitarian vultures. Drag queens doing story hour at the library for small children who have not the slightest idea what is being done to them? Let's have ice cream. Children do not need libertines. They need liberty: they need to lose themselves in the living school of nature.

Here is the novelist George Du Maurier, writing pseudonymously of his own boyhood, in *Peter Ibbetson.* He is an English francophone boy living in a suburb of Paris. At the end of his avenue was what he felt was an "earthly paradise," a wooded park of more than a hundred acres, not tended by any governmental body, nor trussed up with guard rails and overseers. It was, he says, "a very wilderness of delight, a heaven, a terror of tangled thickets and not too dangerous chalk cliffs . . ." And here I pause. The boy in me must pause.

We had a cliff past the dead-end of the street where I grew up. It had a name: Corey Cliff. I have no idea whether anybody still remembers that name. It was about fifty feet high, made up of granite, such stuff as the retreating glaciers left behind while scouring and carving everything else. I never climbed it—I was too small for that, and the cliff really was vertical. A fall from the top would kill you. But on one side, a side that we didn't count as part of the cliff, you could scramble up, getting hand-holds on enormous glacier-tumbled rocks, one of which had fallen like a lean-to upon another, leaving a kind of tunnel or natural hut in between. There my boy cousins and I played. You could not get yourself killed there, though you could probably break a leg or an arm if you were unlucky. My cousins gathered some fine-ground sand there to make cement, for what purpose, I can't remember. I loved the cliff.

Du Maurier continues, directing his attention from the chalk cliffs to "disused old quarries and dark caverns," and again I must pause.

If we look at old postcards, we see that people were once drawn to the ungainly but impressive sights of man's muscular encounter with the land: mines, factories, quarries, derricks. I can hardly imagine a boy who would not like to pick his way among the rusting machinery of an abandoned mill. I was not the most adventurous boy in the world, but I scrambled among the refuse of the coal mines, heaped up a few hundred feet over the main street of my town below. I did it so that I could look at the town from a great height. I did it also to find fossils in the coal, a hundred and fifty of which I brought home, a few every time I went, stuffing the ones I liked best in my jacket pockets. They were of ferns and grasses from who knows how many millennia ago, with even the tiniest veins in the tiny leaves showing clearly. They sometimes had the rusty rainbow colors you see in oil that has leaked from a car's engine onto asphalt. I loved it and learned more about coal and fossils from that refuse dump than I would learn in twelve years of school.

Men had also abandoned things up in those woods, including an automobile and the chassis of a yellow bus with no wheels, which, of course, we duly entered and searched, looking for chance objects that were the more valuable because they were like buried treasure: a nickel, a tattered rag, or a scrap of a forty-year-old newspaper.

And Du Maurier again, moving from the caverns to "prairies of lush grass, sedgy pools, turnip fields, forests of pine, groves and avenues of horse chestnut, dank valleys of walnut trees and hawthorn, which summer made dark at noon; bare, wind-swept mountainous regions whence one could reconnoiter afar; all sorts of wild and fearsome places for savages and wild beasts to hide and small boys to roam quite safely in quest of perilous adventure."

It was not walnuts and chestnuts where I grew up, but carpets of blueberries, moss, and lichen over the bare rocks the glaciers had stripped of topsoil and did not pulverize; and wild roses, blackberry brambles, wintergreen, and white birches such as Robert Frost used to swing upon when he was a boy. Du Maurier's was a "vast enclosure (full of strange singing, humming, whistling, buzzing, twittering, cooing, booming, croaking, flying, creeping, crawling, jumping, climbing, burrowing, splashing, diving things) . . . neglected for ages—an Eden where one might gather and eat of the fruit of the tree of knowledge without fear, and learn lovingly the ways of life without losing one's innocence."

The Heritage of All the World

In 1897, a writer named Williston Fish published a short piece, one can hardly call it a story, called "A Last Will." In it, a wise-hearted and romantic lawyer bequeaths to various kinds of people all the best things that the world has to offer. None of these things can be bought in a store or manufactured on an assembly line. None of them is the result of political action. Here is what Fish's imagined testator leaves to boys, not one by one as he says, but jointly:

> All the little fields and commons where ball may be played,
> all pleasant waters where one may swim, all snow-clad

hills where one may coast, and all streams and ponds where one may fish, or where, when winter comes, one may skate, to have and to hold the same for their period of boyhood. And all the meadows, with clover blossoms and butterflies thereof, the woods with their appurtenances, the birds and squirrels and echoes and strange noises, and all distant places which may be visited, together with the adventures there to be found.

That is not fantasy speaking, but experience and love.

I ask some obvious questions. When was the last time you saw boys playing ball in a vacant field or on a town commons? When was the last time you saw boys swimming in a pond not set aside for the activity and thicketed with rules and lifeguards? I still see boys fishing once in a while, but roaming the meadows to catch butterflies? Exploring hills and mountains and caves on their own, and having adventures that would be written down only in the memory?

If we will not have fiction from Du Maurier, what about the direct testimony of an ordinary boy? Here is Horatio Storer, later to become one of the most famous American physicians of the nineteenth century, the father of gynecology. He was the main force behind the effort to have physicians and politicians recognize the human nature of the embryo and the fetus in the womb, and to have laws drawn up forbidding its murder. That was when he was a young man and still a Quaker, with a Quaker's revulsion against violence. He would soon afterward convert to the Catholic Church. We have an excellent collection of letters he wrote all through his very long life (he was the last surviving member of his Harvard graduating class). In this letter, he is a nine-year-old boy writing home from a boys' school run by Quakers on Cape Cod:

Dear Mother,

I am very well and hope that you soon will be able to get somebody in Lovell's place. I guess you can get almost any sort of a vehicle to come down in. Last Friday the boys went down to Scorten Harbour and staid all day. We made a great fire out of logs and dried beach grass and then we roasted some Menhaden which we had got while the men were seining shad. I should think most a million at a time they are very good eating I think. We sailed most of the way down and back in a fishing boat. I got a cut on the hand which pains me a good deal by a Menhaden which was thrown at me by George Johnson. Give my love to sisters and Father.

Is that a boy's letter, or what? The young Horatio's letters are filled with such adventures, which he relates with a mingling of matter-of-factness and relish. It is clear that the boys were not taken on a field trip by their elders, who no doubt had too much work to do, with preparing and preserving food, keeping domestic animals, washing and mending clothes, tending vegetable gardens, and so forth. The boys go out on their own, exploring the seashore. They stay all day long. They are the ones who gather the logs, probably driftwood, and the beach grass. They are the ones who catch the menhaden, in the vicinity of men who are "seining shad"—notice the technical term. Menhaden aren't usually for human consumption, but the boys don't care, and maybe the fish taste all the better for their having been caught, and for the fresh appetite you get when you are out on the water or on the shore all day long. Horatio mentions as a by-the-way that he got a bad cut on his hand when one of the other boys threw a fish at him, in a burst of boyish high spirits. It doesn't seem to bother him that the boy did that, except that the cut hurts. The school mistress would append a note to this letter, telling Mr. and Mrs. Storer, in these days before antibiotics (1839), that the cut was healing nicely, and that George had thrown the fish with no design to hurt his schoolfellow.

Horatio's letters are filled with description of such spirited outings, and since he did what he did at an ordinary kind of boys' school among a regular little army of ordinary boys, we might well multiply them by a million or two and see them as occurring all over the country. Here he is at ten years old, considerably improved in his mastery of language:

> We had been in a quarter of an hour when Mr. Wing said that as we had not prepared our lessons we might not go to school anymore that day. We went out and in a few minutes it brightened up and began to clear off. A few of the boys were out chopping wood when the question arose, "Who's for building a log cabin?" Some of us went and asked Uncle Joseph about it and he said we might so we went to work some hauling logs others carrying tools, etc. It is now about done. The top is clapboarded over. It has 2 United States flags with a portrait of General Harrison and a picture of his log cabin on them. We intended to have gone to Barnstable if it had been pleasant but it was put off till Monday. At the village several accidents happened a boy broke his leg but I believe there was none beside that of a very serious nature. On Monday we dressed in our best and got into 2 stages and a carry all to go on our intended visit to Barnstable. We stopped at Eldridge's hotel and then went to the bowling alley and staid some time. A good many of the boys then went about some one way and some another. I spent 3 quarters of a dollar while there. At noon we were called together to partake of a dinner. There were 2 large flags which the man said were hoisted to give notice of our presence. A few days ago I saw a paper containing an account of us while there. I went all over the court house then I went up to the cupola where I had a

fine view of all around me. At about 6 we returned home cheering . . .

What happens to a boy's body when he regularly does such things? It becomes supple, strong, energetic, often with no more fat on it than is on a lizard's. What happens to his spirit? It too becomes supple and strong and energetic. The boys here do not need a grownup to direct them. They direct themselves. They do not need someone to show them how to use axes and saws. They know how to use them. They chop and hew and carry the wood. They have even finished the roof with clapboard, and have decorated the cabin with flags and a picture of William Henry Harrison, who would be elected president later that year (1840). Old Tippecanoe must have been a hero of theirs.

Notice the paradox: these are boys who are apparently worked hard at their lessons, especially Latin, and they have regular chores to do at the school, but those things seem not to cramp them but to make them better able to enjoy, in a vigorous way, every hour of liberty they have. So they dress up in their "best"—with all of the social intelligence that that implies—and go the ten miles to Barnstable. How do they get there? Maybe there is a coach, but it seems more likely, because they are waiting for good weather, that they walk those ten miles. Will a boy now walk even a single mile to get where he wants to go with his friends? Then again we notice the boyish matter-of-factness: one of the boys breaks a leg, but other than that, there were no great mishaps. They stop at a hotel, a bowling alley—probably outdoors, that, with ninepins. The boys needn't stick together. They range over the town, and the grownups actually welcome them and celebrate their presence. The grownups do not call the police. They even let young Horatio mount up to the cupola of the town hall, to have a good look around.

Here he is at fourteen, writing to his father:

Captain Attwood would have me stay with him, and so here I am, duly installed. He was very much pleased with the 'Synopsis.' I was very much pleased with him and his wife; they have 5 or 6 young children, all as talkative as can be. He has run a smack up to Boston ever since the Torpedo went, going some 14 times or so, he left off last week and now goes out every night except saturday night catching mackerel in a drag net. On the promontory where he lives, which at high tide is entirely surrounded by water, are some 30 houses whose owners are employed nightly in this business. Hundreds of fish are strewed on the shore among which I notice menhaden, herring, goosefish, smooth and prickly skates, flounders, sculpin, old whiting, and old dogfish; the dogfish begin to come this week. I saw two great shark's heads with smooth teeth, and shall perform the duty of a dentist towards them. There is the skeleton of a whale lying on the beach, which was caught last Wednesday within half a mile of shore, and yielded 50 barrels of oil. Mr. Attwood spoke to me about a species of porpoise which they take in their nets and which I am going to see. There is a Dr. Robinson in the town who is making a collection for some western museum, and upon whom I shall call; he has many skins of fishes, among which is an entire Bone Shark. I shall take a description of it. Tell Uncle Thomas that I made a great mistake in not bringing a gun, as the Captain says I can't find one any wheres down here, and there are birds without number, Plover, Loons, Ring necks, Terns and Gulls, himself to the contrary not withstanding. There are but few birds breed within 5 or 6 miles of here, there are so many houses scattered around; I took a short walk and found a nest scooped in the sand amidst the beach grass with one egg in it; it is either that of a ring-neck or of some kind of tattler, I could not tell which, as both were flying round my head making a great rumpus. The tattler is not the peet-weet, as it is not so spotted, and is darker neither does it shake itself quite so often, but the egg if anything is a little larger than that of the peet-weet; tomorrow I shall try to surprise the bird on the nest and shall then ascertain.

Several things to notice.

The young man is—a young man. He writes with grace and humor. He is "duly installed" in the home of a sea captain, and he delights in the chatter of their brood of children. That bodes well for the physician and obstetrician to come, not to mention the husband and father.

He is passionately interested in the works of nature. He knows fish and sea mammals and birds. He knows their seasonal ways, such as when the dogfish "come in."

He is taking his place as a man among men. He is going to call on that Doctor Robinson, a naturalist. Imagine it: you are a scientist, and out of the blue a boy knocks at your door because he wants to talk to you. Horatio is in indirect communication with his Uncle Thomas, who apparently had recommended that he bring a gun with him, for game. He knows the look and the habits not only of large categories of birds, but of individual species within a genus, distinguishing one kind of shore bird from another. I believe it is safe to say that not one fourteen-year-old boy in ten thousand could now write such a paragraph, though in Horatio's time it might not have been so far out of the common.

It should come as no surprise that Storer, matriculating at Harvard at age sixteen, also not an uncommon thing, would at age nineteen go with other boys and a dog named Tiger on a real voyage with Captain Attwood, to Nova Scotia, Cape Breton, the Magdalen Islands, Anticosti, and Labrador, fishing, hunting, and observing life along the way. Our nineteen-year-old boys can hardly write a letter of any literate sort, or cook an egg in a teflon pan on an electric range.

Let Them Be Born in Wonder

I will now hear an objection, that this sort of thing was all right in the days of Horatio Storer, but is unthinkable in our time, when people do not have to chop wood, fish, or hunt, and when they need not walk from Sandwich to Barnstable, but can take a bus. Also I will hear that the boy from the Quaker boarding school was in no danger, but any child walking more than a block or two away from his house will be vulnerable to kidnappers and molesters, who are in our time as thick as fleas on a stray dog.

Let me say then at the outset that the "progressive" who wants to chain the boy to a desk or to his mother cannot have things both ways. If in fact the world about us is so dangerous that what a boy could do 150 years ago he can no longer do, then we must ask what the difference is, and that difference cannot be that people have more guns now than they used to (they have far fewer, because in Storer's day, every man had a gun for putting food on the table), or that there was a greater presence of policemen back then (people mainly policed themselves). If there are more people in our time who act out sexual or violent perversions, then let the "progressive" explain why, without touching upon the obvious possibilities: the collapse of the family, the neglect of devotion to God, and the general sense that life is for getting the pleasures and the prestige you want. If, however, the boy is *not* more likely to be abused now than then, perhaps because most people are indoors, and there are police and surveillance cameras everywhere, then let them explain what is so wrong about his walking from Sandwich to Barnstable. It may not be what a girl would do; I am not confident in saying so, because I never was a girl. But it is what boys *used to do all the time.* Then why not now?

Here perhaps someone will say, "There is no point to that long walk." I did not know that the liberty to enjoy the natural world around us, to work the body till it is good and tired, and to have nothing but a few coins in your pocket and the clothes on your back as you make your way under the open sky, required a *point:* the reveling in a beautiful thing is its own end. And we may measure liberty not by what some distant governmental entity permits us to do, but by the range and variety of things that ordinary people ordinarily do and without fear—fear of nature, of criminals, or of predatory benefactors, those self-congratulatory good citizens skulking behind the curtains of a house or the windshield of a car, taking photos of you as you idly kick a rock down a sidewalk, or pause by a bush to catch the squeaking and chirping of a catbird. If your streets are empty of children, then your children are not free, and if your children are not free, you are not free.

But there is a point to the adventure, though maybe not a point that we have the capacity to appreciate. The point is to become fully human: in the boy's case, to become a man. So let me tell a story.

A rangy teenage boy, all kneecap and wrist-bone and cowlick, gathers up a little money, buys a Greyhound bus ticket, and rides west from his home in New York till the money runs out. He ends up in North Dakota, sends a wire to his parents to let them know he is all right, and hires himself out to a ranch, working with the cowboys. They take to the lad, even though he has to learn everything, and though he sometimes seemed to lose his wits from about him, gazing up at the bright stars in the clear sky over the plains. There was, for him, nothing better in the world than to sit around the fire with the cowboys after a day of hard work and sweat, drinking hot coffee and listening to their jokes and their stories. He was growing more than muscle and bone. He was growing *soul*.

Why did they not report him to the local police? But why should they? If you look at movies and popular literature of the first half of the twentieth century, you find that they still retain powerful memories of boys who left home to seek adventure, and to build themselves up into men. I have a book, for example, written by the Hall of Fame pitcher Christy Mathewson about a boy who left his callous stepfather after his mother died, and made his way from his native Georgia up to Pennsylvania in the company of his best friend, a black boy who also wanted to seek a different way of life. It is called *Second Base Sloan* (1917), because that is what the young man eventually would become, a crack second baseman for a local semiprofessional team. That would be after he and his friend had worked at all kinds of odd jobs, had shared lean meals purchased with the last nickel they had to their names, and had slapped up a shanty for themselves alongside the bed of a disused railroad. I mention the book because it was the sort of thing that Mathewson, himself a rural Pennsylvania boy from my native county, would have encountered all the time: boys and young men from here and there and everywhere, riding the rails, trading the strength in their shoulders and backs for a job and the pittances that kept body and soul together, making themselves useful in any way they could to any employer they could find, and sometimes—if they had the talent—breaking into a baseball league. Whether they had that talent or not, they could always find what Sloan found in Pennsylvania, namely some local chapter of the Young Men's Christian Association, which at that time was what it said it was, and not a day care center for the children of middle-class mothers, or a pickup joint for gay men.

As late as 1958, American audiences could enjoy looking back upon a time when boys did go forth to take their chances and to be independent, like what the title character did in the movie *The Missouri Traveler*, about a boy (Brandon DeWilde) who goes all the way down to Florida to hire himself out as a farmhand to a man who comes to love him as a son but who does not show that love any too soon (Lee Marvin). I do not think that such stories were peculiar to the America of that era. They are archetypal: Jason sailing with the Argonauts to fetch the Golden Fleece; the young Beowulf and his thanes sailing to Denmark where their leader intends to try his strength and skill against the monster Grendel; Kipling's boy Kim, enlisting himself alongside grown men in the "Great Game" of adventure and espionage on behalf of the British government; Robert Louis Stevenson's lad David Balfour, in *Kidnapped*, saving the life of the Stuart partisan Alan Breck, and braving with him one threat to life and limb after another; or Cormac McCarthy's teenage boys John Grady Cole and Lacey Rawlins, who in *All the Pretty Horses* travel down to Mexico, a land of ranches and horses, of lawlessness and the law that is worse still; of Jean George's boy hero Sam Gribley in *My Side of the Mountain*, who leaves his parents' apartment in New York City to live in the Catskills, burning out a hut for himself from the hollow of a big tree, taming a falcon, fishing and washing and swimming in the streams, hunting for his food, and living the life of a boy's dream.

So there was, I say, nothing strange about what John Senior actually did.

Eventually the rancher found out where his parents lived, and they came to bring him home. He promised to go along, provided that they would let him do the same thing when school was out. They agreed. Such was the young John Senior's first encounter with the hard and bracing world of working men. He went on to serve in the army and to graduate from Cornell, earning a doctorate in English literature. It was his encounter with *reality* that eventually brought him to the Catholic faith.

Here's why. Senior came to learn that the Catholic Church respected the integrity and the goodness of the created order, and that her teachers would say, with Saint Thomas Aquinas, that the grace of God perfects nature rather than supplants it, and that all of our knowledge, including what we know about God himself, comes to us first through the senses. This insistence on *things in their own right* was most congenial to the young man who learned to ride a horse and rope cattle. Things exist, things and not just notions. Kinds of things exist. Boys exist, and they are not girls.

In radical opposition to the regnant educational philosophy of John Dewey, for whom things were of value only for what we could do to them or with them, Senior saw that all creatures were good and beautiful in themselves, prior to any use by man. I will quote here the beginning of one of his favorite poems, "The Starlight Night" by Gerard Manley Hopkins:

> *Look at the stars! look, look up at the skies!*
> *O look at all the fire-folk sitting in the air!*
> *The bright boroughs, the circle-citadels there!*

Look up, behold! But modern man does not look up, and does not behold. He has lost the experience of contemplation. He does not encounter his fellow creatures as endowed with being. He crams his domestic animals into tanks to stuff them with hormones and slaughter them, industrially. He does much the same to his sex and his self. There is a nice connection to be drawn between fatted chickens and fatted children. Or between young people who cannot pick out Venus in the night sky, and young people who know plenty about sex but nothing much about the heavenly Venus, the goddess of holy love.

John Senior came to see that his students could not become sane Thomists, because they had no foundation of experience to build upon. They could not rise up in soul to the Creator of the stars of night, because they had never really encountered the stars of night to begin with. Grace could hardly perfect nature where nature itself was lacking. So, in the most fruitful and counter-technological educational program I know of, the Integrated Humanities Program at the University of Kansas, begun in 1971, Senior and his two colleagues, Frank Nelick and Dennis Quinn, provided young people with both nature and man's first art, his most natural and also most religious art—poetry. They taught them how to sing. They taught the boys and girls how to dance with one another in an ordered and merry way: the waltz. They had them memorize and recite poetry. They brought them outdoors and showed them their way around the starlit sky.

The motto for the program was this: *Nascantur in Admiratione* (Let Them Be Born in Wonder). The wonder is well expressed by the picture on the front page of the program's brochure, sent to me by one of the old students to commemorate the passing of Dr. Quinn. It features a skinny Don Quixote seated atop good old Rocinante the horse. Sancho is nearby. The Don is holding his lance upright against the ground, while he looks up at the stars. The old man had a large capacity for wonder, and it made him childlike, so that all who ever really got to know him loved him, including the squat and earthy Sancho.

That program has borne sons and daughters who have in turn established schools across the country, inspired by Senior's vision. Had it not been for the cowboys and the coffee, I dare say it never would have been. Never underestimate the good to be gained by sweat, work, camaraderie, a bonfire, and coffee.

Dark, not Sallow

If you look at ancient paintings from the lost civilization of Crete, from the second millennium BC, you will notice a peculiar method of distinguishing between men and women: the men are painted with darker skin. Obviously that is not because the men and women come from different parts of the world. The men have darker skin because they spend more time outdoors in the sun. The same is true where my family and I live in the summer, in rural Nova Scotia. The people are largely of French, Scottish, Irish, and Basque extraction. In other words, they do not come from the southern Mediterranean. Yet by age forty, the men have browned themselves into a permanent tan, and the women are still fair-skinned. It is because the men are outdoors, doing work, at all seasons of the year, and I am confident that the women are content that it should be so.

But if you were to take all the men and women and coop them up indoors, those who would suffer the worst from it would be those who are most inclined *not to be indoors,* and if my guess is correct, those would be the men. They would feel like caged wolves. The only way you could get them not to feel so would be by making them content with an absorbing distraction. Many years ago, a highly intelligent boy might be content to brood at the fireside, poring over books. That is not so, now. Now we make the boys docile by setting them in front of screens, playing nerve-shredding video games, or looking at things they have no business even knowing about. They surf the internet when they should be surfing the waves. They chat with friends when they should be chatting with friends, or fishing with friends, swimming with friends, hiking the woods with friends, or playing ball with friends. They are thus lonely without the deep spiritual condition of actually being alone. They know noise but not the deep suggestiveness of sound, blankness but not the wells of silence. They are confined, without the obvious chains against which their spirits might rise in rebellion. They are neutered, and are too much in neutral to sense it.

I believe that life indoors hurts all children, but, as I have said, it does the more harm to the sex that naturally thrives the more outdoors—it hurts the boys. We need not argue that point, though, because whatever we believe about the relative needs of boys and girls as regards outdoor life, it remains true that boys *do languish indoors,* and so it is imperative that we get them outdoors, often and regularly. Their countenances should be ruddy as the young David's was, and not sallow. *Mens sana in corpore sano,* says the poet Juvenal: that is the one thing we ought to beg the gods to bestow upon us, a sound mind in a sound body. Since we are embodied souls, the soundness of the body cannot help but lend its aid to the soundness of the soul, and a body that is exercised among hills, streams, rocks, trees, wild plants, animals, and the good earth, will be more likely to make real the stirrings and aspirations of the soul within.

So did the poet Wordsworth find it, when in his later life he meditated upon what the world was to him when he was a boy:

In November days,
When vapours rolling down the valleys made
A lonely scene more lonesome; among woods
At noon; and 'mid the calm of summer nights,
When, by the margin of the trembling lake,
Beneath the gloomy hills, homeward I went
In solitude, such intercourse was mine:
Mine was it in the fields both day and night,
And by the waters, all the summer long.
And in the frosty season, when the sun
Was set, and, visible for many a mile,
The cottage-windows through the twilight blazed,
I heeded not the summons: happy time
It was indeed for all of us; for me
It was a time of rapture!

And often, when he was skating with the other boys, he would stop suddenly and look at the cliff nearby and the stars that seemed to whirl past him, and he never forgot these things. Which of our children still has experiences like these? Which of our sons knows the rich solitude of the "trembling lake" and the hills? Wordsworth, the boy, was alone and not alone at all, "such intercourse was mine," as he says.

It is long past time to turn off the distractions and meet the world again.

The Man to Follow

What was it about Jesus that drew men to him?

We cannot say that he flattered them. Think of the apostles themselves. Think of the note of weary patience that enters the voice of Jesus when Philip, the slow to understand, after three years of traveling with him and hearing his words, asks him to show to them the Father. "Philip," he says, shaking his head, "have you been with me for so long, and still you do not know that he who sees me sees the Father?"

Think of how much idle chatter Jesus had to endure without rebuke, as that time when the apostles walked with him around Jerusalem and, like tour guides, pointed out the Temple and the other great works, and Jesus said, "There will come a time when of all these things there will not be left one stone upon a stone" (see Mk 13:2). Think of his patience worn thin when the apostles, playing at being his managers, told the women to keep away with their grubby children, but Jesus this time did rebuke them and said, "Let the little children come to me, and do not hinder them, for of such is the kingdom of heaven" (see Mk 10:14).

How rare are his words of praise for his closest friends! Indeed, the one drop of praise, like a cool and all-satisfying drink to a man lost in a desert, is simply that he does call them friends, reserving that praise for the very end—they are not servants, but friends. "Depart from me, Lord," said Saint Peter when he first met Jesus. That was after Peter had followed—perhaps with a muttered curse—the advice of this unknown carpenter to a professional fisherman to go back out on the water after a futile and dispiriting night to cast his net off on the far side. "Depart from me," he said, "I am an evil man" (see Lk 5:8).

Jesus does not contradict him. But he does not pitch Peter back into the lake, either.

If we look to Jesus for machismo, that caricature of manhood, we look in vain, just as we look in vain to his mother, Mary, for effeminacy or hysteria. Boys, and not usually the brightest among them, may be fooled by machismo. Men look for manliness. Women look for it too, in a different way. The boy looks for it without understanding what it is he is looking for. When he finds it, it changes his life. The boy is altogether too apt to reduce manliness to some prominently visible thing, like muscles, or the ability to spin strong cords out of your wrists, like Spiderman, for scaling and swinging from tall buildings. If the boy is to fall in adulation of Jesus, it cannot be by our telling him that Jesus is good, because his mother is good too, or that Jesus liked little children, because his mother likes little children too, and he himself likes them—to tickle them or pull their hair. It cannot be by turning Jesus into an abstraction, because no one falls in adulation of an abstraction. He must be introduced to Jesus the man.

Need I trouble to say that women are not going to do this, at least not in any reliable numbers? The messenger matters, even if we may presume all the good will and wisdom in the world, which in our time we cannot do. What attracts the woman to the person of Jesus is not exactly the same as what attracts the boy. The woman wants from Jesus forgiveness and consolation. The boy wants—even if he does not know it—severity and commandments. The woman wants Jesus of infinite patience and mercy. The boy wants Jesus eager with a baptism that will set the world on fire. The woman wants peace. The boy wants war. They are both quite right to want what they want, and I do not say that the woman will never want Jesus the fighter or that the boy will never want consolation. But the woman who brings to the boy the Jesus of peace and patience and mercy brings to him, without perhaps perceiving it, a Jesus who will not throw open to him the doors of the world, and life. The boy does not want a domestic Jesus. He wants the Lord of the universe. He does not want to hold hands at the altar with a priest and an altar-girl. He wants to swing the thurible as if it were a sword.

Courage, the Foundational Virtue

That is not to say that it is easy to bring that Jesus to that boy. Suppose that we have not smothered the boy's high spirits between the chloroform of school and the dank fever-swamps of evil on the screen. Suppose that the boy is physically boyish, filled with energy and sheer animal spirits. Suppose, in short, that he is the kind of boy made immortal in the first schoolboy book written in English, the eponymous hero of *Tom Brown's School Days* by Thomas Hughes (1857), reminiscing about his own days at the Rugby School from 1834–1842.

You might expect a book about school to have to do with the development of the intellect. Hardly. Hughes' novel is instead about the development of a manly soul: it is essentially a boy-to-man story. When young Tom arrives at Rugby, he is already a boy of considerable "pluck," eager to learn all the traditions of the school, to hold his own, and get into a scrap with anybody who asks for it. He is an amiable scapegrace. We hear about his boxing match with the heavier but less nimble "Slogger" Williams. That match ends, after eight or nine rounds of bloody noses and black eyes and swollen ears, with mutual respect and affection. We hear about how the boys used in their free time to go bathing and fishing in a nearby brook, crossing over to the other side onto property owned by a local farmer, to catch the biggest fish, but making sure that they had no trousers on to get in their way if one of the farmer's hired hands caught them there and they had to swim the brook to escape. We read the play by play of an exciting football match—rugby, in fact, named after the school that made the game famous. There's cricket, and jolly jaunts into town, and feasts, and standing up against bullies, and in general an unstated competition between students and masters, as to who could get the better of whom.

Yet the book is also a warm and admiring tribute to the headmaster of Rugby, Thomas Arnold. Dr. Arnold, father of the great poet and critic Matthew Arnold and the object of his then agnostic son's loving eulogy in the poem "Rugby Chapel," was what we would call an educational reformer, and a man who tried to combine in one person the learning of the Enlightenment and a living Christian faith. I will not discuss here to what extent Dr. Arnold succeeded in that enterprise, but as the master of a school, he stands as one of the leading lights of the century.

Hughes suggests that Arnold knew at all times what reforms he wanted to make, and that he had the prudence to know *how* to make them, working with the nature of the boys so that they would, in becoming men themselves, adopt those reforms as inner directives, workings of their own souls. Here he describes what it was like for a boy to listen to the sermons of Dr. Arnold at chapel on a Sunday: "We couldn't enter into half that we heard; we hadn't the knowledge of our own hearts or the knowledge of one another, and little enough of the faith, hope, and love needed to that end. But we listened, as all boys in their better moods will listen (ay, and men too for the matter of that), to a man whom we felt to be, with all his heart and soul and strength, striving against whatever was mean and unmanly and unrighteous in our little world."

For "mean," understand "base," "petty," "low." How to illustrate? It would be base, petty, and low to pick out the faults of your forefathers while ignoring their virtues and thus not treating them to the gratitude they deserve. It would be mean, sniveling, to bear tales, to ruin someone's reputation, to have someone sacked at work because he expressed a private opinion that was "wrong." It would be low, cringing, contemptible, to join with others behind the scenes in seeking occasion against an exposed and unsuspecting enemy. In other words, it would be mean to do what American schools encourage in their students every day of the week.

Let us go on:

> It was not the cold, clear voice of one giving advice and warning from serene heights to those who were struggling and sinning below, but the warm, living voice of one who was fighting for us and by our sides, and calling on us to help him and ourselves and one another. And so, wearily and little by little, but surely and steadily on the whole, was brought home to the young boy, for the first time, the meaning of his life—that it was no fool's or sluggard's paradise into which he had wandered by chance, but a battlefield ordained from of old, where there are no spectators, but the youngest must take his side, and the stakes are life and death.

The meaning of his life! The very phrase is incomprehensible now. Our young people are taught, usually not in explicit terms but all the more effectively for all that, that there is no meaning in life at all, or, what is much the same thing though prettied up in ribbons, that they themselves are the sources of whatever meaning their lives are to have: Narcissus in love with the nothing that he is. Our young people are taught that "success" is to be measured by the prestige of the college they attend, or the income they earn in the workplace, or by their own good opinion, as they work, Lord help us, "to make the world a better place," fools and sinners who do more harm in the aggregate by their meddlesome restlessness and ignorance than do the more flagrant and obvious plagues upon mankind. If there is any battle, it is against a paper enemy defined by contemporary partisan politics, and so we are left with the most unedifying spectacle of ignorance shrieking against ignorance, pride against pride, folly against folly, all as it were on the sidelines of the true battle, and all of no account.

The boy does not want to be enlisted as an apparatchik. He wants to follow the lead of the man who fights at his side, and who will not be daunted:

> And he who roused this consciousness in them showed them at the same time, by every word he spoke in the pulpit, and by his whole daily life, how that battle was to be fought, and stood there before them their fellow-soldier and the captain of their band—the true sort of captain, too, for a boy's army—one who had no misgivings, and gave no uncertain word of command, and, let who would yield or make truce, would fight the fight out (so every boy felt) to the last gasp and the last drop of blood. Other sides of his character might take hold of and influence boys here and there; but it was this thoroughness and undaunted courage which, more than anything else, won his way to the hearts of the great mass of those on whom he left his mark, and made them believe first in him and then in his Master.

Dr. Arnold did not win their hearts by his kindness, which was, as Tom Brown came to learn later on in his years at Rugby, considerable. He did not win them by his intelligence, also considerable. He won them by his courage.

And courage, Tom will learn, has to do with more than the body and the willingness to fight in a good cause. It has to do with the soul.

We may suppose that the boys at Rugby were all good little Christians who said their prayers and thought daily upon the Sermon of the Mount. Not a bit of it. They were mischievous little pagans who forgot their prayers and thought mainly about cricket matches, hunting, shirking, playing, and feeding. But unbeknownst to Tom, Dr. Arnold had his eye on him and sought to transform the boy's natural courage—when it came to cricket and so forth—into moral courage. So when a boy of delicate constitution, George Arthur, enrolls in the school, Dr. Arnold places him under Tom's care, which proves to be somewhat of an embarrassment to Tom.

Yet Arthur, at first painfully shy, wins Tom over. The boy has lost both his parents to an outbreak of typhus. His father was a man of the cloth, admired in his whole district, who had little enough by way of income, and who worked tirelessly for the spiritual and corporal welfare of his flock. The boy is devoted to his memory, and one of the things that his father instructed him to do was to pray always before bed. So we see Arthur kneeling at his bedside, with one of the bullies in the great room about to fling something at his head, the other boys staring in incomprehension, and Tom ready to intervene against the meanness, but still not understanding why Arthur has to be so different from all the other boys.

But this is all Dr. Arnold's doing. He has made a gamble. Tom is the sort of boy who can tip either way. He can lead the younger boys to ruin, in which case he would have to be sent home from the school, or he can lead them to the qualities of manliness, a Christian manliness. The delicate boy explains to

Tom the promise he made to his father, and suddenly it is as if a new sun had appeared in Tom's universe, or rather it is the old sun, though it had been forgotten. Tom remembers now that he had also promised his mother that he would persist in his prayers, and the memory of that promise, so soon broken and forgotten, gives him pain: for no boy worth his salt will go back on his solemn word. He sees that the boy Arthur has a kind of courage that he has not shown.

When the next night falls and it is time for bed, Tom—in a sweat of indecision, having tried to rationalize his way out of it—goes down on his knees and prays, in the sight of the rest of the boys. And the sky does not fall, but more boys do the same, until in the end those prayers are the norm, and the heedless boys are the exception.

Someone, it is not clear who, said that the Battle of Waterloo was won on the playing fields of Eton. I am not going to pretend that the all-male British "public" schools (they were private) were always models of holiness. C. S. Lewis said, of one such school that he attended as a boy after his mother died in 1908, that the winked-at sodomy between the older boys and the younger ones was among the least of their sins, because in their romantic attachments, the boys sometimes left their worlds of snobbery, ambition, greed, and selfishness. But if we are going to be inspired by Greek poetry, does that mean we must necessarily worship Zeus and indulge in Greek debauches? The one does not imply the other. Courage was of the essence. Debauchery was not. And are we actually to suppose that our sprawling coeducational institutions are not themselves sinkholes of every moral vice, including the one that Lewis named, and this not by the inattention of the masters, but with the full approval of faculty, staff, school boards, developers of curricula and lesson plans, and authors of textbooks? We need not fear that some grubby-minded boys might go to the whorehouse when the alternative is to take up residence there.

Nor should we suppose, by the way, that the authority of the parents will remain unsullied so long as they uphold the right as against the evils taught to young people in school. The very conflict itself will introduce into the child's mind a doubt about all authority. He will be on the road to the great amoral Nothing. Boys are or rather believe themselves to be relentless logicians. They believe that they arrive at their beliefs by reason and not sentiment. If authorities clash, the boys may draw the conclusion you do not expect: that no authority is worth a straw. Do not then put them at that risk. If the school does not affirm the moral vision and the authority of the parents, think of it as you would think of a nest of venomous snakes. Nothing good will come of it.

Holiness in Manly Form

I am looking inside the cover of a novel that used to be read by English-speaking boys and girls everywhere. The book has been dedicated as a gift. It reads, in cursive:

William Reed

for learning Psalm 1 and Psalm 100 and hymn, The Son of God Goes Forth to War

from his S[unday] S[chool] Teacher
Isabelle MacDonald
July 2nd, 1911.

The author's preface ends in a way that the Sunday School teacher would approve:

Should it cause even one heart to feel a deeper trust in God's goodness and love, or aid any in weaving a life, wherein, through knots and entanglements, the golden thread shall never be tarnished or broken, the prayer with which it was begun and ended will have been answered.

M. M. D. [Mary Mapes Dodge]

The book is *Hans Brinker, or The Silver Skates: A Story of Life in Holland*. Mrs. Dodge intended her book also to introduce children to the way of life in that industrious country, and says that the story of her hero, Hans, "is founded strictly upon fact." Hans has grown into his role as the man of the house, because Raff Brinker, his father, was hurt in the head by accident when the levees were breached ten years before, and has not been in his right mind since. We expect that Hans the underdog, living in poverty, will win the Silver Skates by outracing all the other boys, but in fact he does something more manly than that, a lesson that Mrs. Dodge will not let her young readers miss.

There are a couple of things to note here. No author of the horribly named "Young Adult Fiction" would write Mrs. Dodge's sentence; it is too pious and too literate. The sentiments she expresses are heartfelt, and, if I may say, more womanly than manly. When I think of God, my first thoughts are not of his goodness and love, but of his power and glory. Those are not incompatible, just as the man's feelings are not incompatible with the woman's. They are like the very voices of man and woman singing in harmony together, more powerful than if the woman sang alone, and more beautiful and human than if the man sang alone.

I notice that the Sunday School teacher, Mrs. MacDonald, must have asked the boys and girls to commit a hymn to memory, and the one that either she or young Master Reed chose was a robust and manly one:

The Son of God goes forth to war,
a kingly crown to gain;
his blood red banner streams afar:
who follows in his train?
Who best can drink his cup of woe,
triumphant over pain,
who patient bears his cross below,
he follows in his train.

That martyr first, whose eagle eye
could pierce beyond the grave;
who saw his Master in the sky,
and called on him to save.
Like him, with pardon on his tongue,
in midst of mortal pain,
he prayed for them that did the wrong:
who follows in his train?

A glorious band, the chosen few
on whom the Spirit came;
twelve valiant saints, their hope they knew,
and mocked the cross and flame.
They met the tyrant's brandished steel,
the lion's gory mane;
they bowed their heads the death to feel:
who follows in their train?

A noble army, men and boys,
the matron and the maid,
around the Savior's throne rejoice,
in robes of light arrayed.
They climbed the steep ascent of heaven,
through peril, toil and pain;
O God, to us may grace be given,
to follow in their train.

No such hymn that I am aware of has been written in English in the last sixty years, and all the hymns with real fight in them have been stripped from the hymnals: "Christian, Dost Thou See Them," "Fight the Good Fight," "Soldiers of Christ, Arise," "He Who Would Valiant Be," "Brightly Gleams Our Banner," and the old standby "Onward, Christian Soldiers." Instead we imagine Jesus as a louche lover of the effeminate, Jesus not as meek but soft, Jesus not as the stern forgiver of sin, but as the indifferent ignorer of it. And, surprise, boys lose interest in the faith, sensing that it is something for soft people who cannot endure this harsh world and its brute realities of suffering and death. Or they learn that Christianity is all about not being "judgmental." Well, you can spend your Sunday mornings not being judgmental on the golf course or in front of the television or just sleeping in, and you will be spared the eye-rolling embarrassment of silly music to boot.

I will have some more pointed things to say about songs in a subsequent chapter. But holiness in the man's form need not be that of a fighter with fists and clubs, as the "The Son of God Goes Forth to War" itself suggests. There is the holiness of endurance and integrity. Nowhere does the hymn say, nor do I say, that women do not possess endurance and integrity. That is not the point. The point is that the boy is naturally attracted to these virtues when they present themselves in obviously masculine form.

An orphan boy of the streets of India, who cadges food by begging, and who ekes out not much of a life with a woman who sells and consumes opium, one day meets an old man who has traveled by foot all the way from Tibet in search of a promised River of Healing, revealed by a legend about the works of the Buddha from long ago. The old man wishes to immerse himself in that river, wherever it is, because he who does so will be cleansed from all sin and will escape the Wheel of change, of life and all its passions. In the great city of Lahore, this lama is as innocent and as vulnerable as a child.

The boy, who goes by the abbreviated name of Kim, and who knows next to nothing of his mother or father, takes to the old man, begs good food for him, and brings him to the "Great House" of Lahore, a museum of art and all the mysterious and mingled religions of the East. Thereupon the old man, Teshoo Lama, adopts the boy as his "chela" or disciple. This Kim is a finder of ways, a born haggler, a scamp with a winning air, whom the people of Lahore have nicknamed "Friend of All the World," not because he loves everyone, but because he can bandy words in a variety of languages, and can catch the spirit of those with whom he speaks. So the precocious boy and the childlike old man set forth on the Great Trunk Road of India, the old man in search of his River, the boy in search of life itself in all its bewildering ways, and of his very identity. "Kim . . . Kim . . . Kim," he says, as if he were pondering an unfathomable mystery.

Rudyard Kipling's novel *Kim* is another boy-to-manhood story, and central to it is the relationship between the boy and the holy man. The boy Kim is the old man's protection, in more ways than the old man can ever be aware of, but the old man really is holy and wise, and Kim learns from him what he could never have learned from anyone else. Here they are resuming the journey for the river, after Kim—by funds paid by the old lama himself—has spent three years in a British school learning the ways of the Sahibs. The lama and Kim are on the road, and nothing else matters:

> Now and again, indeed, [the lama] would gaze long and long at a tuft or a twig, expecting, he said, the earth to cleave and deliver its blessing; but he was content to be with his disciple, at ease in the temperate wind that comes

down from the Doon. This was not Ceylon, nor Buddh Gaya, nor Bombay, nor some grass-tangled ruins that he seemed to have stumbled upon two years ago. He spoke of those places as a scholar removed from vanity, as a Seeker walking in humility, as an old man, wise and temperate, illumining knowledge with brilliant insight. Bit by bit, disconnectedly, each tale called up by some wayside thing, he spoke of all his wanderings up and down [India]; till Kim, who had loved him without reason now loved him for fifty good reasons.

Such a man alone could make a boy as high-spirited as Kim turn toward the discipline of happy self-denial: "So they enjoyed themselves in high felicity, abstaining, as the Rule demands, from evil words, covetous desires; not over-eating, not lying on high beds, nor wearing rich clothes. Their stomachs told them the time, and the people brought them their food, as the saying is."

The lama teaches Kim that one evil deed is like a stone cast into a lake, with ripples streaming out from the point of impact, breeding trouble after trouble; and the last evil he must repent of is the wounded pride and the anger he feels when a foreigner, a treacherous Russian, tears nearly in two the scholarly drawing of the Wheel of Life that he had worked on, in calligraphy and pictorial parables and commentary, for three years. It is one of the climactic moments of the novel, and Kim must fight—literally fight for their lives against the offending Russian agent and his accomplice. Kim loves the old man, and the old man loves him too, as his son, the best of disciples, even though his Buddhist discipline instructs him against any such strong affection.

Near the end of the novel—I will not spoil things for the reader by revealing the very end—Kim must exercise all of the strength of a man indeed, because the lama is too weak to travel afoot, and must be carried:

> It was never more than a couple of miles a day now, and Kim's shoulders bore all the weight of it—the burden of an old man, the burden of the heavy food-bag with the locked books . . . and the details of the daily routine. He begged in the dawn, set blankets for the lama's meditation, held the weary head on his lap through the noon-day heats, fanning away the flies till his wrist ached, begged again in the evenings, and rubbed the lama's feet, who rewarded him with the promise of Freedom—to-day, to-morrow, or, at furthest, the next day.

Holiness, in a man's form.

Such, and not in a work of fiction, was Father Flanagan, whom I have mentioned already, to the toughs who came to Boys Town from all kinds of usually miserable places and conditions and misled lives. Flanagan always insisted that there *were no bad boys*, because they were still boys and had not hardened into bad men. Boys have a sixth sense to sniff out the hypocrite, the phony. One boy, Eddie, puts Father Flanagan on the spot. He says that he *is bad,* and that if Father Flanagan believes otherwise, he is just a liar. Eddie tries to win the point by mentioning one bad deed after another. Flanagan will not give in. After he says a mental prayer that God will inspire him with just the right words to say, he turns the tables on Eddie and asks, "A good boy is an obedient boy, right?"

Eddie agrees, with wholehearted contempt.

"Does only what his teachers tell him to do?"

"You bet!"

"Well, that's all you've ever done, Eddie. The only trouble with you is that you had the wrong teachers—wharf toughs and corner bums—but you have certainly obeyed them; you've done every last wrong and rotten thing they taught you to do. If you could only obey the good teachers here in the same way, you'd be just fine!"

That argument wins the boy over. But it is not a simple war of logic. The argument persuades because of the man doing the persuasion. It is not that Eddie sees the answer as you might suddenly understand that if two fives make ten, twenty fives will make a hundred. The answer is *embodied in a man,* one who is like Eddie the boy, and yet who captures his allegiance by means of his wisdom and his love. The boy follows Father Flanagan's logic because he follows Father Flanagan himself.

Fatten the Flesh, Starve the Soul

My home town, whose population for a hundred years hovered around five thousand, gave to the Catholic church some fifty priests and a hundred religious sisters over the course of eighty-five years. The men were what Fr. Paul Mankowski has called "broad-shouldered baritones," able to hold the attention of other men and to enlist dozens of town boys into the ranks of assistants at Mass. One of them, a Father Thomas Comerford, used family money to build a three-story parish hall so that the coal miners in his congregation would have a healthy place to go to after their grueling days underground, rather than just the saloons. There was a reading room there, a bar, a room fitted out with a pool table, various meeting rooms for the many social and beneficent clubs, mostly all male or all female, that a typical parish would boast in those days, and, on the third story, an auditorium with a stage and lights, the area in front of the stage doubling as a basketball court. I am looking at a photograph of Father Comerford, in November of 1918, leading a mile-long parade down the main street of my town to celebrate the recent armistice. He is small of stature but grave and intelligent, and he ruled the parish and the town itself with a kindly iron fist.

Men fall in love with women, but boys fall in admiration and emulation of the man who can make things happen, and if that man is holy, they learn the ways of holiness sometimes without even suspecting it. To say, as does the Jewish boy at his bar mitzvah, "Today I have become a man," is to acknowledge that you do not have to give up your manhood to become holy; rather, there are forms of holiness that we recognize as markedly masculine, and then to be the more devout is to be more, not less, of the man. It is not to belong to what George Bernard Shaw, in his atheistical scorn, called the "third sex," that of a clergyman. It is not to be effeminate and sly, advancing your sacerdotal career by gossip, toadying, and having the right taste in clothing, food, and wine. It is to be like the energetic and fearless Saint Isaac Jogues, or Saint Damien of Molokai, or Saint Francis Xavier. Sanctity, then, is not comfort but danger: or comfort, because there is danger. "Take up your Cross and follow me," says Jesus.

Need I press the point that we have robbed boys of almost every hope that they might see masculine holiness at work in their churches?

Or manliness, with a touch of the holy, in their ordinary lives.

Work to Do

In his autobiographical sketch of his youth, *Prairie-Town Boy,* Carl Sandburg describes in often humorous detail the variety of jobs he held from the time he was about eleven years old. He shined shoes, cut hair, delivered newspapers, swept and cleaned in a store, hauled and packed blocks of ice, printed a newsletter, delivered milk, milked cows, washed bottles, scoured ovens, maintained railroad ties, was a short-order cook, washed dishes, weeded gardens, picked out potato bugs, "cleaned" bricks from demolished buildings for reuse, ran a boathouse, raised curtains and did backstage work at the Galesburg Opera House, and baled hay. That was to earn odd money, in part to help the family while his sister Mary was going through high school, which Carl himself *did not do.*

It did not include the chores he had to do around the house, all necessary if a family was going to live well rather than go to seed. For example, when he was still a pretty small boy, his father sometimes during the summer had to lower him down by a rope into the well so that he could shovel out the silt that had built up in it over the year. He was also, as the oldest boy, the main pumper of fresh water as needed, and that meant sometimes priming the pump with rain water they collected in a cistern, or, in winter, running back and forth from the well to the kitchen to get water heated at the stove, pouring it on the pump to thaw it out so that the handle could be moved. Winter also meant taking the wash out to the line to dry, and having the clothes freeze while you were doing it. "Coaxing those frozen pieces of cloth to go around the rope clothesline to be fastened with a wooden clothespin," he says whimsically, "was a winter sport with a challenge to your wit and numb fingers in Illinois zero weather, with sometimes a wild northwest wind knocking a shirt stiff as a board against your head."

Basically, the whole young life of Carl Sandburg was taken up, when he was not in school or church, with working hard, usually outdoors, and playing hard, outdoors and in all seasons. It is really not possible to reckon up how much he learned about persons and things and the world from that work of his, but it surely lies behind his famous description of Chicago, which used to be a city alive with the sweat and the smell of men doing work that was the heart's blood of the nation:

> *Hog Butcher for the World,*
> *Tool maker, Stacker of Wheat,*
> *Player with Railroads and the Nation's*
> *Freight Handler;*
> *Stormy, husky, brawling,*
> *City of the Big Shoulders.*

The city is crooked, wicked, and brutal, and Sandburg answers yes, it is true, it is that, but it is more, and it raises its head over the "soft little cities," and laughs as a young man laughs, "Laughing the stormy, husky, brawling laughter of Youth, half-naked, sweating, proud to be Hog Butcher, Tool Maker, Stacker of Wheat, Player with Railroads and Freight Handler to the Nation."

Sandburg is not excusing the wickedness and brutality. He is celebrating the life.

Nor do we need the city for work. When Father Flanagan of Boys' Town was a six-year-old boy in Ireland—Eddie, as he was called—it was his job on the farm to see to it that the cows did not wander into the bogs and the sheep did not blunder against the briars and get entangled. Once when that happened, Eddie went to the sheep and began disentangling the thorns from the wool, which had to be saved. The job took a long time, and the boy's hands were bleeding freely, but he carried that sheep away on his shoulders, little man that he was, and saw his father kneeling and saying prayers of thanks, for the good shepherd that the lad was to become. For the father had been a patient witness of that good work.

It will accomplish nothing if we merely raise boys who are not crooked, not wicked, and not brutal, at the expense of life itself. Better a live man than a dead thing. Better the work of a living being than the functions of an apparatchik. Better a hearty and dangerous laugh than an empty or ambiguous smile. So let us now turn to the boy and his work.

Precocity in the Shoulders

The scene is a farm house on the shores of the great Lac-Saint Jean in the interior of Quebec. The soil is rich, but the climate is forbidding, and the long winters are the constant subject of conversation for the farmers from October to May. A young man from a nearby farm has come to pay a call on the Chapdelaine family, particularly because of Maria, whom he loves, but whose heart he has yet to win. He owns and works that farm with his brother. He and the Chapdelaine patriarch, Samuel, speak of their work, and are joined by Samuel's son, "Ti' Be," "Little Bert," who is quite simply one of the men now:

> He smoked and talked with the men now by virtue of his
> fourteen years, his broad shoulders and his knowledge of

husbandry. Eight years ago he had begun to care for the stock, and to replenish the store of wood for the house with the aid of his little sled. Somewhat later he had learned to call Heulle! Heulle! very loudly behind the thin-flanked cows, and Hue! Dia! Harrie! when the horses were ploughing; to manage a hay-fork and to build a rail-fence. These two years he had taken turn beside his father with ax and scythe, driven the big wood-sleigh over the hard snow, sown and reaped on his own responsibility; and thus it was that no one disputed his right freely to express an opinion and to smoke incessantly the strong leaf-tobacco. His face was still smooth as a child's, with imma-ture features and guileless eyes, and one not knowing him would probably have been surprised to hear him speak with all the deliberation of an older and experienced man, and to see him everlastingly charging his wooden pipe; but in the Province of Quebec the boys are looked upon as men when they undertake men's work, and as to their pre-cocity in smoking there is always the excellent excuse that it afford some protection in summer against the attacking swarms of black-flies, mosquitos and sand-flies.

The author, Louis Hemon, is simply writing about what he has seen: these French Canadian pioneers are the men and women he lived and worked among and grown to love most dearly. We could wish to have more novels from Hemon, but he was struck by a train in Ontario, and died at the age of thirty-one. *Maria Chapedelaine* is his lone masterpiece.

It is absurd to suppose that women and girls did not also work, very hard, at tasks that were essential for the survival of the family. In *My Life with the Eskimo*, Vilhjalmur Stefansson says that in the far north of Canada, a grown man without a woman could hardly scrape by to keep body and soul together. Clothes had to be mended constantly; a woman's needle was as valuable to the Eskimos as a gold mine would be to us. Food had to be prepared and fires kept going. The wife would have to *chew the soles of her man's boots* when he was off with his other pair, to make them soft again, because one day out in the terrible cold would freeze them solid and make them of no use at all. The women on the Lac-Saint Jean also worked constantly, and indeed the climactic decision at the end of *Maria Chapdelaine* has to do with work. The heroine Maria is loved by two men. One of them is fairly well off and lives now in Boston. He holds forth for her a life of plenty and ease, of dancing and continual social events. The other is the neighbor farmer. He holds forth for her the forbidding life of a woman on a farm in the same heartbreaking place where she has lived all her life. Maria chooses her people, her land, and the suffering.

So I do not want to imply that work has to do with one sex and not with the other. But I do believe that we must try to restore to boys a kind of work that will mark the passage from boyhood to manhood, and make them into men whom any man would trust: building courage, self-reliance, self-sacrifice, perseverance, and a willingness to put the needs of others before one's pleasure or vanity. Here I turn to a fine novel by Paul Annixter, the pseudonym for one Howard Allison Sturtzel (1894–1985), a writer of books for children back in the day when parents could be confident that such books were not exercises in sexual ideology. The novel is called *Swiftwater,* and is about a teenage boy, Bucky, who lives with his parents and his sister outside of the town by that name, right on the border between the habitable and the uninhabited northlands of Maine. His father, Cam Calloway, does a little farming, but mainly he hunts and traps, selling the pelts with an eye toward paying off the mortgage on the heavily forested area where they live.

Sturtzel was like Sandburg and Hemon: he described things that he knew, that he himself had experienced. He had to "ride the rails," as Sandburg did when he was seventeen, traveling here and there to pick up odd jobs and send money back home to support his grandmother and his mother. He lived for a while alone in northern Minnesota so that his descriptions of bogs, of swift-running streams jammed up with the logs of fallen and rotten pine trees, of the habits of the weasels, foxes, bobcats, and wolves, read like a true hunter's travelogue.

In his novel, the boy and his father are setting traps along a no-man's-land of ancient boulders, unmarked forest, stream, swamp, mountain, and ravine, when the father, crossing one of the logjams, accidentally dislodges a large boulder from above, which lands on his leg and breaks it. Bucky must run the miles back to civilization to get help before his father freezes to death—and this too, after his father instructs him on how to set the leg temporarily by main force, splinting it and binding the splint and encasing the leg in a makeshift cast of rounded shells of pine bark. But with the father now unable to work, Bucky himself must go and be the family's support, out in the woods alone, yet not quite alone, because he brings with him all that his father has taught him over many years, about the habits of animals, how to shoot a rifle, why you should take life only when you need to, what kinds of traps to set and where, how to build a lean-to, how to skin the animal, or butcher game upon the spot—everything. Bucky must even spend the occasional winter night, in subzero temperature, in a self-made "wickiup" in the forest when he is too far north along the trail to go home.

He goes out alone for the first time and discovers, to his dismay, that the traps have caught animals, but the animals are not there—only their bloody remains, including the remains of a porcupine, which some vicious beast has devoured, quills or no quills, leaving a spotty trail of blood from its own ravenous jowls. One after another, Bucky sees his traps spoiled, and then he comes upon the beast, the "bad dog" that one of the Micmac

Indians had warned his father about. It is a wolverine, a male, three and a half feet long, and utterly vicious.

The boy has to track the wolverine, because his family's welfare depends upon those pelts: no pelts, no food this winter. He follows the blood and the stink of the beast right into a regular tangle of dead trees and snow, where all the advantage is with the wolverine—and there he slips and the rifle falls useless, eight feet below him. He swings his ax at the attacker, and the blade draws blood, but the tough hide and the muscles of the wolverine are proof against it. In the end, after the beast has bitten through the boy's leg and caused his trousers to soak with warm blood, Bucky takes his skinning knife and buries it in the beast's neck. A wolverine: "Off in the black woods a wolf howled dismally and Bucky smiled. Never again would the night dogs make his skin crawl. Never again would he be afraid of anything above ground."

We teach "pride" in our schools, but pride in what? When Bucky comes home with the skin of the wolverine, his father insists on pegging it to the wall of their cabin for everybody to see. The author's comments are measured and wise: "Pride rose in him like a yeast over Bucky's exploit, for none knew better than he the craft and mettle of this demon beast and all the boy had overcome in the valley—things that would never come out in words. Pride glowed in Bucky, too, a quiet and tempered thing that steadied and strengthened like strong food in the belly, for it had its roots in things conquered and achieved."

This is not narcissism. It is not a selfish and childish parade. It is not arrogance. It is not the deadly sin. It is a confidence that is "quiet and tempered." It does not puff the boy up; in fact, after the deed, Bucky becomes quieter than usual, focusing ever more intently upon the work to be done for his family. This confidence is like food. It is based upon *something done*.

Knowledge in the Hands

Now I turn to comedy.

The scene is a schoolroom. The twelve-year-old children have been given an assignment to write a letter to a friend "on some subject of general interest." Naturally the teacher calls upon the most reliable students first. These are a girl and a boy—a boy whom the other boys don't like very much. The girl has written one about the town's courthouse. It is entirely programmatic and prim. "It is four stories high," declaims Miss Raypole in perfect complacency, "and made of stone, pressed brick, wood, and tiles, with a tower, or cupola, one hundred and twenty-seven feet seven inches from the ground. Among other subjects of general interest told by the janitor," and so forth. One boy, Penrod Schofield, begins to go into a half-conscious daze, twisting a button on his shirt.

The next performer steps up. It is the model boy, Georgie, and he has decided to polish an apple for the teacher, writing his letter as addressed to *her*. "I thought I would write you about a subject of general interest," he says, "and so I will write you about the flowers. There are many kinds of flowers," and so forth. Penrod lapses into complete sluggishness. At that point the teacher calls on him, and he gets up, fog in his brain, and reads his composition, which was the letter he snatched up from his older sister Margaret's dressing table, because naturally Penrod hasn't done his assignment.

He gets up uneasily. He has not the slightest idea what is in the purloined letter.

"Dear friend," he declaimed. "You call me beautiful, but I am not really beautiful, and there are times when I doubt if I am even pretty, though perhaps my hair is beautiful, and if it is true that my eyes are like blue stars in heaven," at which point Penrod loses his breath and the class erupts into delighted laughter.

Who says that boys and school are enemies hard to reconcile? Everybody says it. Booth Tarkington, the author of the scene above in *Penrod and Sam*, said it. But the irony is that Penrod Schofield has more imagination, not always of a benevolent sort, than any ten other children put together, imagination that usually involves the hands: *doing* rather than *talking*. In the course of this uproariously comic novel, Penrod and his friends build a ramshackle tree hut, fish an angry tomcat out of a cistern by using one of the boy's trousers for the cat to climb up (with dire results for the trousers), chase a stray horse into an empty barn and try to feed it there by stealing fruit and vegetables from their parents' cellars, filch from one of the boys' uncle's attic an instrument they use as a tuba but which actually is a rare artifact from the reign of Louis XV, stuff empty lady's stockings with wood shavings and a cat to make a five limbed monster—such things. And behold, the girl that Penrod likes best gives him the credit for turning a dance into complete mayhem, when for once Penrod was totally innocent, and says, whispering it into his ear, "I don't believe there's any boy in the whole world could of done *half* as much!"

We know these things, don't we? And yet we have now created the worst of all worlds. Our young people know how to do very little, *and* we have banished from the curriculum the content and the ideals of the old classical learning. So our students are now not only ignorant of books but ignorant *by means of books:* by the bad books they read or pretend to read, and by the many things they could be doing, which the books and interminable assignments and visual and electronic distractions keep them from doing. We are raising a generation of people who are overschooled and unfit for real intellectual work, *and who are not practiced in the hands,* unfit for that kind of imaginative work that involves doing, not talking.

This has hurt boys especially badly, because boys, slower of speech than their sisters are, and blessed or burdened with a metabolism that cries out for action, and somewhat more leisurely in physical and intellectual development, grow used to an unnatural and misleading situation, one that they are quite literally *schooled into.* Show me a boy who gets bad grades in school, and I can make no inferences regarding his intelligence. He may be a dunce, or he may be a genius, or he may be an ordinary boy for whom the stuffy classroom, characterized by a film of niceness over a regimen of what seem to him to be senseless and obnoxious rules, is a hell on earth, and a hell all the hotter, or colder, if much of the instruction specifically aimed at his sex tells him that he is brutish, stupid, unreliable, and gross. If one boy out of twenty hates school, the problem is with the boy. If nineteen out of twenty hate school, the problem is with the school. The problem is made all the more vicious in our time, when boys are portrayed as losers, and girls are encouraged in a kind of sparkle-sprinkled pride that boys and men in ages past would have found, for their own sex, insufferable and even delusional.

What would happen, though, if we gave the boys intelligent things to do with their hands? What would happen if we raised boys to be what is called "anti-fragile," working at a variety of tasks that will stand them in good stead the rest of their lives, and learning in their hands and shoulders from their very errors, just as muscles are built and bones are hardened by the risk of a good football game? Father Flanagan at Boys Town knew what he was doing. That wise place featured all kinds of shops, for repairing automobiles, baking, hair cutting, printing, wiring, carpentry, and so forth. This ought to be a common thing, and for boys all along the range of intellectual power.

I am looking at a reprint of William B. Stout's *The Boy's Book of Mechanical Models* (1917). The reprint is prefaced by a telling publisher's note to the effect that "there are two problems with this book." The second problem is that the models require a lot of cigar boxes and wooden spools, objects far more common in the home in 1917 than now. The first problem is that the book "is far from being politically correct," as "it dwells fondly on stereotypes."

In fact, Stout does almost no dwelling fondly upon anything, stereotypes or otherwise. What he assumes is that a lot of boys like to make mechanical things with their hands and with tools. Actually, he does not assume it. He knows it, from wide experience. "The ideas included in this book," he says, "have been collected during a number of years of work among boys." That is not what he supposes boys might do but what he knows very well boys have done and would do. Indeed, the boys themselves share in the authorship of the book, as Stout says he "wishes to thank the boys who have worked with him in the past for their share in the inspiration of this volume, and offers it to other boys of America in the hope that they may obtain from its pages an enjoyment equal to that he has had in its preparation." Stout's hope is social as well as technological: "Give the real boy some tools and a workshop, and half the problem of bringing up the next generation is solved."

Them's fighting words now! But in what other society in the history of the world would those words have been the slightest bit controversial? Name one. There aren't any. Why then would we hesitate? If boys in school are languishing, and for a variety of reasons, not one of them doing any credit to us, *why not try something else*, especially if that something else has had a history of success?

The book is almost entirely made up of diagrams, drawn up with extreme precision, and instructions. Here is a typical section from instructions on how to build a toy phonograph to play records already made. Stout has explained in a few plain sentences the principles upon which the phonograph works, and—given that the boy has a record to play, and has purchased a few Victrola needles—he will now show the boy how to construct the turntable, the armature, and the "horn" with a diaphragm of paper, mica, or isinglass to register the sound vibrations. In these sentences, he is describing the mechanism that holds and directs the needle:

> The wheels O and X are about three inches in diameter, and the heavier the better. The pulley on the shaft g below, shown at P in *Figure 4*, should not be more than three-quarters of an inch in diameter. The shaft g is mounted in the frame F, f, *Figure 1*, between bearings made of needles, *Figure 4*, the lower needle from the lower end of g passing through a hole in a small stick a, fastened to the base A, with its end resting and pivoting on a piece of tin or glass t. This is shown in the sketch of the "balance wheel."

If you do not think that a boy in our time could follow 250 pages of such directions, for building, among other things, a model motorbus, a shadow picturescope, a model elevator, a perpetual calendar, an air-line railway, a gutter water-wheel and dam, a walking policeman, a wooden elephant, a writing telegraph, or a submarine boat, the question is simply, why not? Stout's book was tremendously popular then. The nature of the boy has not changed. What has changed is his intellectual, physical, and spiritual diet: he is being starved.

As so often, some things are hard to see because they are too big and too near. Stout tells the story of a young man who was so gifted, he could do anything, so that the first we hear of his genius, it was as a boy when he took up the lute. His father then sent him to school to be a physician, and he could have done that too, but something else seized his interest:

> In 1583, while he was standing in the cathedral at Pisa—you have doubtless read the story in school,—he saw a bronze lamp which was suspended from the ceiling by a chain swinging back and forth, and he soon noticed that each swing took the same amount of time, whether the lamp swung through a wide arc or a small one. He immediately applied the idea to a small machine,—somewhat in the nature of a clock,—made to measure pulse beats. He had no knowledge of arithmetic or mathematics, or he might have gone farther with this invention at this time.

The lad in question is Galileo, and Stout intends to show the boys how to construct a pendulum clock based upon Galileo's discovery. I like that offhand comment, "you have doubtless read the story in school," when now it is almost certain that boys and girls *have not read the story in school.* But if we have let down our political guard, both men and women will find the story to be interesting *and not at all strange:* it is exactly the kind of thing that an intelligent young man might do. When Blaise Pascal's sister said of her young brother that he played with conic sections the way that other children play with toys, again, if for some reason the apparatchik of political orthodoxy is nodding or indisposed, we say of course, that is just what a boy genius would do. It does not surprise. It delights.

Some boys—I think we can justly infer this from the habits of boys across cultures and through the ages—learn about complex ideas and their interrelations by "seeing" or "handling" and manipulating, turning them this way and that, *and not by means of verbal description.* Think of the Rubik's cube. The worst thing you can do to them, if we are talking about mathematics, is to compel them to *use words to describe what for them is essentially non-verbal or beyond words.* It drags them down. It impedes. It frustrates. Stout's book is spare on the words and generous with blueprints, including close-ups. Give the boy a dead car and have him take it apart and try to put it back together again. Strange? Boys did that sort of thing everywhere in the developed world. We are the strange ones. Give him an old lawn mower and tell him the same. Give him saws, drills, hammers, a router, a plane, a drill-press, a lathe, a grindstone, a block and tackle, screws, bolts, and plenty of wood and old metal. See what happens.

Give him an old bicycle you pick up from the heap at the dump, or you buy for five dollars at a yard sale. Tell him that you will give him a prize if, with screwdriver and wrench, he can take the bicycle apart and put it back together, and explain how the brakes and the gear-shift work. Ask him also to examine the difference between engaging one gear or another; this he might do by placing the bicycle upside down and rotating the pedals by hand to see what happens, and to feel, in his hand, the difference in effort it requires to make the revolutions, and to see, right before his eyes, how much "payback" there is for the effort in this gear or that.

Perhaps the boy will make the leap from Stout's whimsical toys to the real things, and then he or he and his friends together might profit from a book like *Audels Carpenters and Builders Guide #4* (1923; my reprint is from 1946). Theodore Audel and his company published guides on electricity and plumbing and other fields of skilled trade; I am taking this one as an example. It is impossible for me to convey the full power of such a book. The complete set of guides runs to over fifteen hundred pages, most of them illustrated with diagrams of machines and their inner parts, designs, cuts, and geometric figures. To say that most high school students would be baffled by them is an understatement. Not one college student in twenty, I am persuaded, would find them comfortable to read, if they would understand them at all. You have to be able to see three dimensions in two, and to rotate objects in your mind, and draw conclusions from mathematical premises—while understanding at the same time that a material like wood is not steel, and so you must allow for imperfections, "crooks," swelling, and drying.

I am looking at a page in a chapter on how to build stairs, one of the easier sections of the book. The page has six diagrams on it, described thus, under the heading "Theory of hand railing": "A and B, plan and elevation of section of a cylinder; C, plan diagram of a wreath enclosed by tangents; D, development of tangent planes in elevation; E, face mould diagram; F, sketch of the prism shown in C."

That is pretty simple stuff by comparison with the long chapter on Mill Work, describing in great detail a wide variety of machines: mortisers, tenoners, jointers, lathes, planes, sanders, rabbeters, band saws, scroll saws, borers, and moulders (machines for fashioning moldings). A diagram of a borer shows all of its many interrelated and organized parts: spindle stop, counterweight, spindle, operating lever, belt shifter handle, ball thrust-bearing, friction disk, self-centering chuck, tilting table, degree scale, tilting screw, raising clamp, drive shaft, tight and loose pulleys, and frame. "Essentially," says the editor, "a borer consists of *a vertical spindle having a chuck at one end and telescoping a splined sleeve which engages a drive pulley, the assembly arranged to rotate in bearings attached to the frame of the machine.*" The clean smell of machine oil and sawdust warm from the saw—and no political posturing, no dabbling in a swamp of feelings, no aim other than to do good work with good tools. Imagine a clever boy with the machine, and the guide to help him understand it, and plenty of scrap wood to work on—and time, precious time, truly free time away from the chloroform of the school and the jittery distractions of the internet.

I won't leave the book without citing a long account which departs from the plan of diagram, description, and instruction. It has to do with the making of wood itself, that is, the transformation of trees into lumber:

> Prosy description can give little idea of the spectacular and strenuous activity of logging forces at work in the woods. Horses and men rushing to and fro, seemingly in constant and imminent peril of falling trees; giant logs, with skidder cables attached, plunging through the undergrowth on their way to the skidder, there to be tossed into the air and whirled dexterously into place on the log cars; the "boom-boom" of falling trees, the roar of steam exhausts, engines puffing, workmen shouting warnings and instructions—all contribute to a medley that makes the forest seethe with motion and resound with a confusion of notes.

Why should we care about how the lumber is made? For the simple reason that you ought to know your materials, and it helps to understand why what you experience with your hands has an explanation in nature. "Density of growth," says the reporter, "the frequency with which high winds may visit a certain locality, climate and soil—all have an influence on the structure of wood in trees, and all these conditions are considered by the lumberman before he begins operations for the manufacture of lumber." Let the boy then learn *why* pine is used for studs, and what kind of pine, and why oak has the qualities it has, and what it is good for, and why the old-timers used hemlock for flooring, and cedar for shingles and shakes.

Same for working with metal. What is the difference between iron and steel? What is the advantage of a copper roof, and why does it acquire that green patina? Why is silver used in mirrors and cameras and bells? What is platinum doing in a catalytic converter? What, for that matter, is a catalytic converter? Why did they make light bulb filaments out of tungsten? What is the difference between a wood screw and a sheet rock screw, and why are the screws made so?

Same for working with electricity. What is a fuse? What is a resistor? What is a transformer? Find a plan for the making of an electric bell, or something else that works by means of an electromagnet and a current that rapidly goes on and off and on and off. *Do things. Make things happen.*

A Hierarchy of Tasks

Some scientists attribute differences in male and female behavior to the pressures of survival over many thousands of years, winnowing away those behaviors in each sex that are not well adapted for the climate, the food supply, and the protection of your group from predations by beasts, including those that walk on two legs (see, for example, the work of the anthropologist Lionel Tiger, *Men in Groups*). I claim no expertise in sociobiology. I notice two things. One is that no sane person ever says that male and female wolves, to take an example, behave as they do arbitrarily. We say that they *must be so*, because otherwise the wolves would die out. The second is that men are astonishingly similar to men and women to women across cultures, at all stages of technological development, in all climates, and with all manner of religious beliefs and customs. So if someone were to say to me, "You have a limited view of masculinity," my response must be, "I would like you then to show me some masculine trait that I have missed, that shows up everywhere, in all cultures, from the Vikings to the Patagonians, from the stone age to the space age, from the tundra to the tropics." What is it that I have failed to note that is to be found among the Homeric heroes and the men of the Norse sagas, among the legendary Zulu warriors and the schoolmen of the Middle Ages? Most people, when they make that objection, do not imply that the trait they are looking for *is certainly to be found* in boys and men everywhere. They simply want it to be so right now. But then they are in danger of wishful hoping, or of ignoring the good that is in front of them, in favor of some other characteristic that is not.

Here is one feature of masculine life that does show up everywhere, and it bears heavily upon the raising of boys. Men in groups organize themselves by a hierarchy of tasks. Not a *variety, but a hierarchy.* We are not talking about doing three things at once. We are talking about doing three things at once that are organized hierarchically so that it is actually one unified thing and not three. I will mention that it is the only way certain kinds of things can be done at all. Without it, you cannot hunt animals that are big, dangerous, or fast; men cannot outrun a deer or wrestle down a wild ox or out-fight a boar. Three or five men together cannot do it. But three or five men doing different things in different places, coordinated, can surround a herd of deer, or can maneuver the ox into trouble, or can harass the boar and drive him against the man ready to spear him. Again I stress that we are not talking about mere variety, since some actions must be ancillary to others, and the thing to be attained is not equality or "fairness" in who gets to make the kill, but brute success. We are certainly not talking about "cooperative" work, mainly involving talking and talking, and smoothing over differences, and settling into an acceptable mediocrity. That sort of thing is no good for girls, and boys find it either insufferably tedious or downright detestable. They bristle. Or they shrug and let the big talkers talk, because they are insufficiently interested in consensus. It does not inspire.

Watch what boys do. You have seven boys and a football. The odd boy, usually the biggest, plays quarterback for each team. Here he is with the three boys of one team, huddled around him. His palm is spread out, and he traces patterns on it with the index finger of his other hand. "John, you line up to the left. You run straight ahead for four steps, fake a cut to the left, then run straight across to the right as fast as you can. Dave, while he's doing that, you line up on the right, and just when John is coming across here, you make as if you are going to stop, but then run deep straight ahead. Louie, you line up to the right of Dave, and run hard but then double back toward me. I'll throw to Louie as a backup. The pass is going deep to you, Dave. Let's go!" And of course the other team lines up, having agreed as to who is going to cover whom, and all the boys are clear as to what down it is, and what the boundaries of the field are, and what counts as ending the play (one hand touch, two hand touch), and what the score is, and whether there will be field goals. It is the most normal thing in the world, so much so that we do not even notice it.

But it is *like the kind of work that men in groups do, and it is like the objects they make.* That is, the organization of men in groups to do certain complex tasks resembles the character of the things to be accomplished by the tasks. Men organize themselves hierarchically, and thus create objects that are also organized hierarchically. Consider these objects: a sawmill along a river; the frescoes on the lives of Mary and John the Baptist, in the Tornabuoni Chapel of the church of Santa Maria Novella in Florence; the play *The Tempest*; and the Constitution of the United States.

The sawmill is essentially a large machine that lends power to a variety of other coordinated machines, with men stationed at a variety of places to do a variety of things. It is the touch-football plan, or the snowball fight attack plan, writ very large. If you visit such a place, you will be impressed not simply by the enormous individual pieces of the mill, such as a many-toothed wooden gear weighing eight hundred pounds, or a ten-foot-long reciprocating saw, but by the kind of mind that could conceive of the whole at once. The power of falling water, which requires a dammed-up river, spillways to keep the flow relatively stable, and a turbine to be turned by the water, is transformed into rotary motion, which is then transformed by complicated arrangements of gears and belts into rotary or reciprocating motion at speeds that can be controlled by the workers, as there are "clutches" to shift gears, so to speak, or "neutrals" to dis-engage a machine entirely from the power. We are not talking about, let us say, forty people working next to one another, each at his own task, or about forty people getting together to share ideas about a single task, but about a mock-organism, whose units work as wheels within wheels, as subordinate clauses within subordinate clauses. And some of the characteristics of the hunting party are here too: the danger to life and limb, the gravity (literally!) of the aims, and the bold attack upon some-thing in the natural world that is hitherto oblivious to man. In this case, it is the river, the man-defying stones wherewith the dam and the works must be built, the huge trees required to make gears so large, the iron ore that must have been quarried in a mine and smelted in a foundry by teams similar to those that work in the sawmill, and the raw material to be worked on by the machines.

Shift the scene. It is Florence, in 1485, and Domenico Ghirlandaio has received a commission to execute new fres-coes in the chapel of the rich Tornabuoni family. He is not a sole painter. That was not how frescoes were done. He has a large and thriving studio, which means that he employs many men; he and two of his brothers and his brother-in-law, and a dozen or so young men, including one boy named

Buonarroti—Michelangelo Buonarroti. Again I must stress the precise character of the work to be done. It is not that you have a big wall, and that you allow each of the painters to execute some portion of it, a little bit here and a little bit there, as he pleases, with but the mildest of subordination, so that maybe the Master gets the most prominent parts, as the faces of Mary and John. It is also not that Domenico polls the grown men for their ideas, and opens up discussion to the boys.

Subordination—hierarchy—is of the essence. The Master's is the idea for the whole. He and his brothers will execute the *cartoons,* that is, the huge sketches, on paper, of the plan. The actual painting will be done by the entire studio, but in strict order, because the nature of the fresco requires it. You have to prepare the surface for the paint, which must be applied while the plaster is still fresh: hence the term *fresco.* That means that some people will be working on the plaster, sometimes on scaffolding. Others will have to be making the colors, pounding them in a mortar. Since the young men are affiliated with the studio for the purpose of instruction, the Master will in fact give them certain areas to paint, not as they please, but within a certain range of what the Master pleases, and the younger they are, the more likely they will be doing things preparatory or ancillary to painting, rather than wielding the brush themselves. They work as an army.

The probably autistic Michelangelo was unusual in later life, in that he often worked alone, though if you look at the Sistine Chapel ceiling, you see not just one painting next to another, but a vast and hierarchically conceived whole, as if there were forty Michelangelos working simultaneously, not each at his own task and not all together at a single task, but as, so to speak, Michelangelo the private obeying Michelangelo the sergeant obeying Michelangelo the lieutenant obeying Michelangelo the general, who subordinates himself to the requirements and the glory of the thing to be done; and in the series of paintings itself, we see the whole story of the human race subordinated to the dominant painting, that of the creation of Adam, with the greatest span of non-painting in the history of art, namely the space between the commanding finger of God and the finger of the man, as God imparts to him the spark of life—of the divine intellect. In all of this, we find not equality but hierarchy and self-similarity, like the small carvings upon the capital of a pillar in a Gothic cathedral, as if each tiny portion of the cathedral were itself a cathedral, or pointed toward the cathedral as a whole in its small and unique way.

The scene is a garret in London, in winter, and a man is leaning over a sheet of foolscap, dipping his pen in an inkwell and considering. Several things are on his mind at once. He is thinking of the Advent readings from the Book of Common Prayer, as they refer to the coming of the Christ-child and to the second coming of Christ in glory to judge the quick and the dead. He is thinking of the startling news that everyone in town is talking about, a report of the miraculous survival of some shipwrecked British men in the Bermudas. He is getting on in years, and though he has been notably successful, he is beginning to tire of the hard work, and so is thinking of making a kind of farewell to the stage. His last two plays combined motifs of the two great Christian feasts, the Nativity and the Resurrection of the Lord, and this play will be no different. He is a loyal English subject, though a somewhat secret Catholic, and as such he has long meditated upon the nature of authority, and the dangers of abdicating it in favor of a sentimental trust in human goodness, or to pursue one's pleasures rather than submitting to the severities of rule.

He is thinking of his company of actors, including the boy genius for whom he has recently written two astounding parts; he will give him a third. He is thinking of each actor, his strengths and weaknesses, and he is thinking of himself as an actor too, because he is actor, director, manager, and playwright in one.

If we were to mull about in the scraps of paper around him, we would see something odd. He evidently is not working from start to finish. We have a set-speech here, a song over there, the beginning of a scene from the middle of the play, and what looks like the epilogue. He is working not linearly, from one point to the next, but holistically, on many things simultaneously, and on things to be subordinated one to another. "I will have the buffoons," he says, "team up with the monster Caliban in a treacherous attempt to kill Prospero and seize the island," and thus to reflect in burlesque form the main action to which theirs will be subordinate, namely a treacherous attempt at assassination, which itself will be subordinate to the action that precedes the play and sets the moral stage for it, namely the usurpation of Milan by Duke Antonio in alliance with the king of Naples, subordinating Milan to Naples. . . . And there are wheels within wheels, eleven men on a field doing eleven things at once that are all organized hierarchically to one end, a screen pass to the wide receiver, drawing the enemy into the defile between the mountain and the lake called Trasimene, driving the flock out against the hill where the bowmen are posted, raising the bridge hundreds of feet in the air, in filaments of steel.

"I shall begin with the storm itself," says Shakespeare, and proceeds to write a short scene in which all of the main motifs of the play are raised, though the modern ear, not used to thinking of literature as architectonic, finds it hard to hear them. "I shall raise the issue of authority, and proper obedience," and so he does, turning the tables on the noblemen aboard the ship, and giving the audience a complex and subtle analysis of hierarchy and how it works and why it works. "Tend to the Master's whistle!" cries the tart-tongued and hearty Boatswain, because in the hurly-burly of the storm, words are hard to hear and feelings are of no consequence; you have to catch the head coach's signal immediately, the call of the bugle, the lilt of the conductor's baton, and act accordingly; the whistle gives instructions according to the notes the master plays on it. "I shall have the noblemen get in the good Boatswain's way," says the playwright, "and then we will see what obedience is all about when they try to give him orders where orders from them are out of place." Then there will be another form of obedience too, and another hierarchy: prayer.

"Old John will make a fine Boatswain," says Shakespeare, smiling.

The Tempest is a different kind of literature from what we are used to, the discursive and often meandering novel; it is more like a cathedral than it is like a story with a beginning, a middle, and an end, although it has those, too.

And then we have the Constitution. It is not meant to be a cultural document. It is a blueprint for the rules of a game, or for the workings of an intricate machine. Think of the old provision regarding the election of senators, who are (we must excuse the comedy, but it was the original intention of the Founders and their intention for a long time enjoyed some actual realization) supposed to be repositories of cultural and political memory, meant, as in ancient Rome, to act as a brake against the sometimes unruly and heedless passions of the populace and their direct assemblies. We might think that such important men would be chosen by the people themselves, but no, they were to be selected by the legislators of the individual states, and not two at once, but one at a time, staggered over the senatorial terms of six years. That meant that the states *as states* would hold one hammer over the national government, while in almost all other respects the national government held the hammer over the states. Or consider the strange provision that each state would be represented by two senators, regardless of population, while in the larger body, the House, the apportionment would follow population. That meant that small states—which could be quite large in area and quite critical for the health of the nation; think of the rather sparsely populated states that provide us with most of our wheat and corn, and the even more sparsely populated states that provide us with most of our minerals for industry—would not simply be swallowed up by the influence of the large states, as is the case among the Canadian provinces. A simplistic ideology of fairness for the individual voter is here made subordinate to a more complex vision of the common good, which demands that *ways of life, visions of the good, and contributions to the nation* be respected in their several forms.

We could go on with this kind of analysis. Why are the rules of baseball what they are? To the uninitiated, the rules seem arbitrary, often picayune. Why is the pitcher not permitted to drop the ball while he is standing on the pitcher's rubber with a man on base? What is the big deal if the ball slips from his hand? Why is a foul bunt with two strikes a strikeout, but if the batter swings and hits a foul ball, he is still alive? Why should a ground ball that passes over third base be fair even if it lands in foul territory beyond the base, while a line drive whistling over the base, landing in foul territory, is foul? Why must the batters keep to a certain order in the lineup? Each rule is subordinated to the good of the game. They are crafted as ingenious devices, often balancing one another, to provide for an equitable and interesting game, rewarding skill and speed and power, but also allowing for the excitement of sheer luck.

Make War, Not Nice

The structure of school right now combines the worst of two worlds: regimentation without war and without any great and difficult task to be accomplished, and talking much, without the grammar of reason to aim the talk toward the truth.

I will leave the reader with a scene.

It is New Orleans, 1849. An eleven-year-old boy is playing chess against his uncle, who knows the game very well. The boy, however, is like Mozart: he can conceive of many motions simultaneously. It is not just that he can follow along, in his mind, a string of moves, so that if his uncle does this, he will do that. The vision is global, so to speak.

"Paul," says the man, knitting his brow, "are you really going to let me do this?" It is early in the game, and the boy has allowed his uncle to move a pawn all the way into the sixth rank, on the queen's side, where there is a rook missing. The boy's father has been boasting about him, and the boy, playing white, has spotted his uncle that rook.

The boy shrugs and glares at the board. He is absorbed. He allows the uncle to take another pawn, so he is now down a pawn along with the rook.

"Paul," says the man, a few moves later, "I have you. We'll exchange queens," he says, as he takes the boy's queen, threatening his sole rook and an immediate checkmate. The boy shrugs again.

"Check," he says, moving his bishop against the uncle's king. The uncle begins to worry. He moves the king forward. The bishop is protected by a knight, protected by the threatened rook.

"Double check," says the boy, moving the knight and revealing the rook. The uncle's only move is to take the bishop. The boy is now down a rook, a bishop, and a pawn.

"Checkmate," says Paul Morphy, taking his uncle's rook in the corner.

Paul Morphy was a boy genius, self-taught, learning by watching his father and his uncle play. He was the "Newton of chess," as the master Aleksander Alekhine would call him. At age twelve, he would play the master Johann Jacob Loewenthal in a tournament and dismember him. To this day, people say that in the quick development of pieces and in the wide open game, nobody has improved upon the principles that Morphy discovered.

There have been other untaught boy geniuses of chess (Raul Capablanca), and untaught boy geniuses of mechanics (Thomas Edison), and various other things. My point here is not that every boy is a Morphy waiting to be discovered. It is instead to suggest that the *kind of learning* that the boy may very well prefer is shown in strikingly clear form by such boys as Paul Morphy.

What do we have to lose? Play chess, backgammon, gin rummy, poker. Put a musical instrument in the hands of the boy and keep him away from sentimental slop. Give him a pile of wood and blueprints. Give him pulleys and a block and tackle. Let other boys join him. Say, "If you can dig and set the foundation for your hut, I will provide the shingles and the lumber." I used to know two boys who turned the basement of one house into a great plain for the re-enacting of famous battles, with chalk to mark the terrain, and toy soldiers, and dice for the chances and changes of the fight. After they played the battle indoors, they would take up toy weapons and do the same thing over outdoors.

Wheels within wheels, gears interlocking with gears, the tight end slipping through the slot for a quick pass, the front line giving way to lure the Romans forward while the flanks encircle them at Cannae, an electric circuit that cuts off as soon as it is engaged and then turns on again as soon as it is disengaged, knight to king's rook eight; let the boys be boys, and let them work and learn.

Songs to Sing

When Jesus had broken the bread at the Last Supper and shared the wine—instituting the sacrament of the Eucharist—and commanded his apostles to go and do the same in remembrance of him, he and they proceeded to do something else *in remembrance.* They sang a hymn (see Mt 26:30).

They did not have hymnals at hand, or a garish projection of the words upon the wall in front of them. They had the hymn in the memory. Where else would it be? There was no printing press. Scrolls were rare and precious, and books were laborious to produce. Yet people had songs in their minds and hearts. The Jews had their great collection of hymns, the psalms, which are Hebrew poetry of the highest order. Many of those psalms come down to us with abbreviated instructions at the beginning: "To the chief musician" (85), "A song or psalm for the sabbath day" (92). We may suppose that there were melodies associated with each, and that these too would be in the minds and hearts of the people. If it seems implausible that anyone should know by heart a hundred and fifty melodies, I call to my reader's attention the fact that there are plenty of old Christian hymnals, for congregations that could not afford better, which include only the words of the song and the name of the melody; many hundreds of such in a single book. Then too there is the fact that even when you have a hymnal with the full score, many people cannot or do not read the music anyway.

Music—poetry, meant to be sung—is the universal heritage of mankind. No society before ours has been deprived of it. I do not mean the products of mass entertainment. I mean music and poetry that a people really do possess, as heirlooms, as precious vessels of meaning, of human desires and sorrows, of laughter and merriment, of tears and memorials, of honor and praise, and of supplication before the divine. All people until our time have had that. The illiterate pagan Germanic tribes had it, and they sang the deeds of gods and heroes long past, and in fact archaeologists have sometimes unearthed proof of a battle or a deed memorialized in poetry that was finally written down several centuries after the event. The Greeks sang of Troy, and Troy really did exist, but had been leveled to the earth six hundred years before Homer ever composed his epic poem on just a few days in that long, long war.

We are the odd ones out here, a people without songs, without a cultural home. I do not exaggerate. Ask yourselves which songs you can expect a teenage boy, his grandfather, and the next door neighbor all to know. If the answer is one or two, or none at all, then you have proved my point.

It was not always so. Even for boys—*even?*—it was not always so.

One of the things that Carl Sandburg says that he and his pals did, on a summer evening when they felt like it, was to sing. They sang in harmony: two of the boys did the tenor parts, and he and another friend covered the baritone and bass. When Satchel Paige, late in his career after the color barrier had been broken, pitched with the Cleveland Indians, he and three of his teammates made up a barber-shop quartet, and would regale the fans behind home plate in the hour or so before the game began. Satch sang bass. Every all-male college in the nation had singing groups, most of them made up by the boys on their own initiative. I have seen a booklet of the songs of one of those schools: *Carmina Princetoniana: A Collection of the Songs of Princeton College* (1873), a hundred pages of patriotic, pious, romantic, hearty, jaunty effusions of young manhood. The best-known is a Latin song in praise of relishing life—even academic life—while you can:

> *Gaudeamus igitur,*
> *juvenes dum sumus!*
> *Gaudeamus igitur,*
> *juvenes dum sumus!*
> *Post jucundam juventutem,*
> *post molestam senectutem,*
> *Nos habebit humus,*
> *nos habebit humus.*

> *So let us rejoice while we are young,*
> *so let us rejoice while we are young!*
> *After merry youth*
> *and troublesome old age,*
> *The earth will hold us at last,*
> *the earth will hold us at last.*

The Welsh have had a long tradition of all-male choirs. I have in my hands a collection of Welsh hymns, printed in both Welsh and English, for use by immigrants from Wales to the United States. Many of the hymns are markedly masculine, as for instance the rousing "Gwyr Harlech," "Men of Harlech." Here is the first stanza of the English rendering—it is basically a separate poem in English, inspired by the matter and the manner of the Welsh:

> *Men of Harlech, march to glory,*
> *Victory is hovering o'er ye,*

Bright-eyed Freedom stands before ye,
    Hear ye not her call?
At your sloth she seems to wonder,—
Rend the sluggish bonds asunder,
Let the war-cry's deafening thunder
    Every foe appal.
Echoes loudly waking,
Hill and valley shaking,
Till the sound spreads wide around,
The Saxon's courage breaking;
Your foes on every side assailing,
Forward press with heart unfailing,
Till invaders learn with quailing,
    Cambria ne'er can yield.

How old is the song? As old as the last great Welsh attempt to resist incorporation into England: the so-called seven years' siege of Harlech Castle (1461–1468). The "Saxon" in the song is the Welsh way to describe the English—*Saesneg*, in Welsh, preserving a cultural memory that goes all the way back to the invasion of the Christian British Isles by the barbarian Germanic pagans from across the North Sea, pushing the true British into and across the western mountains. That is also the source for the legends, preserved and embellished in Wales and Brittany, of a lost Christian kingdom ruled by King Arthur and his short-lived fellowship of the Round Table. "Men of Harlech" is sung to a stirring march, full of energy and passion. You cannot possibly sing it slowly, or with a lilt. It is music to fight by. The masculine rhythm, with abrupt and strong shifts, like sudden punches to the chest or the head of an opponent in a boxing ring, fit the male "tempo," with its bursts of adrenaline and its quick return to calm. You cannot squeeze enough femininity out of that melody to bat one eyelash.

It should not be controversial to say that if you gave such a song to boys, their hearts would beat the quicker: it would be a joy to them. That, of course, is why they never will sing such a song in our schools now.

Music Hath Power

When I play hymns on the piano, and I am a very poor player, my dog Jasper will curl up at my foot that works the pedal, and will stay there, completely content, until he senses that I have finished. Sometimes one of the cats will perch on the table behind me, and all at once I feel a nudge against my back. It's the cat, with that cat behavior that says, "I am happy."

"Music hath power to soothe the savage breast," says Shakespeare, and he is not original in saying so. The ancient Greek myth of Orpheus tells the tale of the poet and singer who went down to the underworld with his music, lulling the ferocious three-headed dog Cerberus, and calming all the hearts of the guards down there, until he came to the king and queen of hell themselves and asked for the soul of his beloved wife, Eurydice, to return with him to the world above. The queen Proserpina granted the favor on condition that Orpheus not look once at Eurydice until they were out. So Orpheus and Eurydice made their way forth, until just at the entrance of hell Eurydice slipped and Orpheus looked back—and lost her forever. Pitched into sadness, Orpheus retreated to the wilderness, shunning all converse with women, and doing nothing but playing on his lyre and singing sad songs, and none of the beasts would molest him, such was the power of his music.

The tale would end badly for Orpheus, but the point is crucial. "The touches of sweet harmony," to use Shakespeare's words again, are not for pretty decoration. They are touches of tremendous power. The poet Amphion, in Greek mythology, was said to have raised up the walls of Thebes by song. The poet Arion, according to legend, was thrown from a ship by wicked men, but he had his lute with him and he played, and dolphins came to his rescue, letting him ride them safely to land. Plato understood the power of music, and that is why he said that all education was at base a musical one. For music is expressive of a harmony between body and soul. It appeals most directly to the seat of rational or irrational passions, depending on what kind of music we are talking about. There is all the difference in the world between a man who knows what to do and has the heart to do it, and the man who knows what to do but will not do it, because he lacks the courage, the *chest*, as C. S. Lewis would call it in *The Abolition of Man,* following Plato's lead in the *Phaedrus* and the *Republic.* "The good man," says Plato, "is the only excellent musician, because he gives forth a perfect harmony not with a lyre or other instrument but with the whole of his life." Good music builds the chest.

Bad music lets the chest cave in. Plato said that the first sign of decay in a commonwealth would be a radical change in the people's music. An elderly minister once told me, and my experience confirms it, that when a congregation is about to go bad, the first thing to be corrupted will be the music.

It isn't hard to see why. We are aware of the beat of the heart, and the regularity of our breathing. We do not speak in a flat monotone but lend to our voices the rising and the falling that mark the beginning, the middle, and the end of a complete thought. Our voices have tones and overtones for the imparting of meaning and intentions that words themselves cannot carry: think of the many ways in which someone might say the three simple words "I love you." To sing is more than to say. It is to declare, to put your heart into it, to blazon it across the skies. We might recall here Plato's analogy in the *Phaedrus*, comparing the soul to a charioteer with a pair of horses, one wayward and ill-tempered, the other noble and strong. The appetite, the belly or groin, is represented by the wayward horse, and a faculty we have ignored in all of our current education, what Plato calls "spirit," Greek *thymos*, what we might call "heart" or "guts" or "drive," is represented by the noble horse. The charioteer, rational though he may be, can get nowhere without the power of those horses. If he does not direct them, he will never attain to that vision of beauty he has once beheld and with which he desires to be one. But he can only control the bad horse through the agency of the good horse. The head rules the belly through the chest, said Lewis. Otherwise the belly, or the region further south, will rule, and the head will be mainly employed in finding excuses for the groin. We have raised a generation of hypertrophied heads in the service of bellies, with sunken chests and skinny arms unable to do a thing about it.

Music is then for the building of that heart, that chest. The Greeks understood it, though Plato did not agree with the particular music which formed the education of the Greek boy. That was primarily the songs of the epic poets, Homer and Hesiod. All education worthy of the name is essentially a musical one: it calls upon the Muses. So the Greek boys in their gymnasia would learn geometry, and would train their bodies in the arena, and would recite and hear recited songs about Achilles, Agamemnon, Ajax, and Odysseus.

It is one thing to know what the right thing to do is. It is another to remember it in the heat of the moment. It is still another, and the critical thing, *to do what is right*. Secular people have often told me that they do not need religion to tell them what is right and wrong. I doubt that, because I am not deceived by the world they have created, wherein an overlay of etiquette can hardly conceal a yawning moral chaos beneath. But let us concede the point. Let us grant that you do not need anything but your reason to tell you that it is good to lay down your life for your people. Let us grant that the egg between your shoulders is quite sufficient to tell you that it is good to admire the beauty and the virtue of a good woman. Let us grant that you can appeal not to Emmanuel but to Kant to see that you should not tell a lie even when telling the truth will set your livelihood or your very life in the balance. Do we not see the problem? It is almost the difference between knowing *that* a person named John Smith exists, where he lives, what he does, how tall he is, how much he weighs, and whether he is married, and *knowing* John Smith himself. The moral knowledge, to be really effectual, must inform the whole being and not just the theoretical calculator.

If you want a definition of courage, you can ask your boy to get out a dictionary. But if you want your boy to *be courageous*, you must embody that courage in action, and, apart from the crises that call for courage, your best opportunity comes in song.

Scores that Build the Soul

What songs do our boys sing now?

As soon as I ask the question, I am aware of a strange state of affairs. That is, most of my readers will assume that *boys hardly ever will sing anything at all.* I assure you that that is an anomaly of our time and place. We are the oddballs. If you look at a summer photograph of an ordinary group of boys from any town in America, in 1950 or 1920, you will notice right away, as I have said, that these boys have spent almost all of their time outdoors. You will see it in the complexion and in the muscles of the neck and wrists. Well then, as the soft body and the thin wrist is to what any boy would be like if he spent most of his time outdoors climbing trees and playing ball, so the boy with no songs in his heart and mind is to what any boy used to be in the days when music was not mass-produced, and when schools actually taught poetry that people had cherished for generations.

If you go to Florence and you look at the choir loft sculpted for the cathedral, especially that portion of it carved by Luca della Robbia, you will see what I mean. Della Robbia has included in his sculpture a couple of panels of choirboys. One group of five, three older boys and two younger, are crowded around an open book held by one of the smaller boys. They lean forward, looking over shoulders and singing together. If you look closely at the tilt of their heads, the shape of their open mouths, and the size of the body, you can tell that they are singing in harmony: they are *not singing the same notes.* In front of them is a female figure, perhaps an allegory of sacred music herself, playing a lute, and on the other side of her, three more adolescent boys, singing from a long scroll that the two boys on the ends hold open. That would surely be a scroll for the music of a chant. Because you do not want to be flipping pages during a prayer, the more elaborate chants, which might have as many as three or four hundred notes, would be printed lengthwise, horizontally as it were. Those boys are then probably singing *in unison.*

The boys would not have just showed up once in a while to sing, when they felt like it. They were undoubtedly trained. For a while, in the Florence of Della Robbia, there were even confraternities of adolescent choirboys organized for the social, moral, and spiritual welfare of the members. But wherever you went in Europe, for many centuries, if you heard polyphonic music from the choir loft, you were listening to men and boys. Let me stress what that means. Johann Sebastian Bach composed cantatas and motets almost weekly for the churches of Saint Thomas and Saint Nicholas in Leipzig. He composed them specifically for boys to sing the soprano part and sometimes the alto part. Every choral piece by the great Palestrina required boys for the singing. The same goes for all of the polyphonic composers of sacred music, for hundreds of years. By the time of Georg Friedrich Handel, in the eighteenth century, women were taking the soprano parts that required years of training and a mature voice, and yet the boys remained a crucial part of the music: you cannot sing *Judas Maccabeus* without them. Think of that. For hundreds of years, countless works of art of the highest order required, for their realization, the participation of children—of boys. And they were not just there for decoration. In a male choir with men and boys, it is the children, the boys, who sing the highest part, who soar and carry the most memorable strands of the interwoven melodies. The men are in supporting roles. The boys take the lead. As in the climactic moment of *Judas Maccabeus,* when a choir of boys greets the victor over their Greek oppressors who had desecrated the Temple:

> *See where the conquering hero comes!*
> *Sound the trumpets, beat the drums!*

What boy would want to sing such words? Rather, what boy would not want to sing them? You may know the melody, by the way, as it has been used for an Easter hymn, missing from all contemporary Praise 'n Worship and Songs R Us hymnals:

> *Thine is the glory, risen, conquering Son!*
> *Endless is the victory thou o'er death hast won.*

But is this a thing of the past, merely? I am looking at a photograph of nine young men, taken outdoors, near the woods. They are grave in their mien, and look as if they could, if necessary, put the hurt on anyone so foul as to give offense to a woman or to abuse a child. Two are holding guitars, one holds a banjo, another holds a Celtic drum, and still another, in the center of all, holds an accordion. Four of them are there, apparently, to lend their voices, or perhaps they simply do not have their own instruments with them. They are students at a boys' school in Pennsylvania, Saint Gregory the Great Academy. All the boys at Saint Gregory's play rugby and soccer, all of them learn to juggle (at which they are stunningly proficient), all of them serve at Mass, soldier-like, and all of them learn to play music and to sing. Their juggling and riding of unicycles aside—perhaps, *the other three things, for boys and men, have much in common.*

I cannot do better than to cite the instructors at Saint Gregory's themselves:

> At the academy the students learn and sing both traditional folk music and sacred music, but music is not just an important part of their daily routine—it informs all they do. Apart from music classes and rehearsals, the boys sing for Mass, Morning and Evening Prayer, at leisure or banquets, in the vans and during athletic events. They sing about love, war, brotherhood, heroism, villainy, humor, sadness, joy, and God Almighty. In fact, it is hard to think of any aspect of their experience that is untouched by music, and this is precisely why their education at the academy is so precious.

What might boys sing? What men have sung. They have sung about brotherhood and heroism: hence "Men of Harlech," above. But here is a song particularly about a lad's heroic determination to follow in the steps of his fathers:

The minstrel boy to the war is gone,
In the ranks of death you'll find him;
His father's sword he has girded on,
And his wild harp slung behind him.
"Land of Song!" said the warrior bard,
"Though all the world betray thee,

One sword at least thy rights shall guard,
One faithful harp shall praise thee!"

The Minstrel fell! But the foeman's chain
Could not bring that proud soul under;
The harp he loved ne'er spoke again,
For he tore its chords asunder,
And said, "No chains shall sully thee,
Thou soul of love and bravery!
Thy songs were made for the pure and free;
They shall never sound in slavery!"

The author of the song, the poet Thomas Moore, com-posed it in memory of his fellow Irishmen who had fallen in the rebellion of 1798. The folk melody is sweet but rousing, with an unusual minor key modulation in the third last line of each stanza: *Though all the world betray thee,* and *Thou soul of love and bravery.* What does the song teach? Loyalty, love of coun-try, courage, even in the worst of odds. What difference does it make if you are alone against the whole world? But what man is worth his salt if we cannot imagine him standing alone for what is right and just? "One sword at least" shall he raise in defiance of the wrong. If we must be overcome, let us go down fighting.

Courage is often shown more movingly in defeat than in victory. The minstrel boy falls, but he takes his wild harp with him. Recall the Babylonians who begged their captive Hebrews to sing to them songs of Israel in a foreign land. "By the waters of Babylon we sat and wept," says the psalmist. The minstrel in Moore's song is dying, but he will not give the Babylonian English the pleasure of playing music on his harp. He tears the strings apart: the harp, which is the "soul of love and bravery," shall never "sound in slavery." And so the song ends—in death that is yet triumphant. The sentiment is that which J. R. R. Tolkien found so moving, and made of it a leitmotif for the darker movements of his *Lord of the Rings* trilogy. As it is put in *The Battle of Maldon,* which Tolkien cited:

> *Thought must be the harder, heart be the keener,*
> *Mind must be the greater, while our strength lessens.*

The very poem from which those brave words come shows the chasm between us and all other cultures that have ever flourished upon earth, or rather between us and a real culture. The Anglo-Saxon chronicler, having described the circumstances of a battle between a hastily mustered English militia and a crew of tribute-seeking Vikings, ceases from his prosaic description and inserts a song, several hundred lines of which survive. For hundreds of years that is how our linguistic ancestors recalled and handed on to their children great deeds of courage: they sang them.

The essential boy has not changed. The body is the same, the heart that stirs within, the bones and the blood, all the same. What has changed is the music, the starveling diet or the poison he has been given. Show me what music the boy listens to, and you show me his soul, or what his soul is in danger of becoming. If he has no music at all, you show me a soul that has not yet quite come to birth. We do not want such men, if we heed Shakespeare:

> *The man that hath no music in himself,*
> *Nor is not moved by concord of sweet sounds,*
> *Is fit for treason, strategems, and spoils.*
> *The motions of his spirit are dull as night,*
> *And his affections dark as Erebus.*
> *Let no such man be trusted. Mark the music.*

Songs of Love

What is the difference between saying something and singing it? We say that birds sing, but we might be engaging in an equivocation when we say so. The birds send forth signals in cheerful melodic form. Mister Mockingbird, singing during mating season to mark out his territory, will lose around a quarter of his weight in a half a day, which he then must make up by some ferocious eating, till it is time to attract and impress Miss Mockingbird all over again. When April comes, I hear the loud throaty piping of the oriole, a single note, usually, then silence, then the note again, and perhaps again, and then a burst of song. What that signifies in oriole-communication, I don't know. I know that most birds have a variety of calls which they use in different circumstances. The wheezy squawk that we associate with the blue jay is actually a serviceable signal, telling the other jays that there is a crow nearby. He has a different wheezy shriek for the presence of a hawk. Thus is the blue jay, nest robber though he is, incidentally helpful to the smaller songbirds, which also "understand" the call.

That is not what human beings do when they sing, and that is why I think that the verb is equivocal. We will yell or moan or gasp as signals to others that danger is near, but when we sing, we give artistic *form* to our thoughts and words and passions, a form that helps us leave the mere imparting of what is called "information" far behind. "Information" so called is usually not *formed* at all, but left as a bare statement. "I believe that Annie Laurie is physically attractive, and I would do anything for her if she would return my love," says the Scotsman, and Annie knits her brows and glares and turns away. "Singing is what the lover does," said Saint Augustine. If you are not in love, you are not going to sing. Singing is *for love,* as it is also *for worship:* we sing to express what ordinary language cannot convey.

Let us then suppose what every healthy culture known to man has supposed, which is that boys grow up to be men, and men take wives. During that long period when boys are far more comfortable around other boys, and very much need to be with them for their intellectual development, they are also and always still boys destined to become men, and so while we shield them from sex, we also rightly nudge them in the direction of married love. We would be grossly irresponsible not to do that.

Well, that is just what ordinary and sensible people used to do, probably only half aware that they were doing it. Here is the first stanza of the poignant love song I have alluded to above:

> *Maxwellton's braes are bonnie,*
> *Where early fa's the dew,*
> *And it's there that Annie Laurie*
> *Gave me her promise true.*
> *Gave me her promise true,*
> *Which ne'er forgot will be,*
> *And for bonnie Annie Laurie*
> *I'd lay me doon and dee.*

What does the boy learn when he sings a love song like that? He learns that the love of a good woman is more precious than rubies, as the sage of Proverbs says. He puts himself in the place of a gentle and faithful man who understands how great is the gift that Annie Laurie made when she gave him her promise true. He learns—he will feel it thrill in his bones—that his place may be to lay down his very life for the woman he loves; it is a sacrifice at the heart of the drama of the sexes.

He also learns to love beauty in its distinctly womanly form:

> *Like dew on the gowan lying*
> *Is the fa' o' her fairy feet,*

And like winds in summer sighing,
Her voice is soft and sweet.
Her voice is soft and sweet,
And she's a' the world to me,
And for bonnie Annie Laurie,
I'd lay me doon and dee.

Not throwing punches in a strictly segregated women's division of boxing, not shrieking at a political rally, whereof we have altogether too much and from both sexes, not mugging and bellowing like oxen, but she moves gently, mysteriously, like the summer breeze, and "her voice is soft and sweet." Says King Lear in the final moments of his life, mourning over the body of his daughter Cordelia, "Her voice was ever soft, / Gentle and low, an excellent thing in woman." Boys might not in their bumptious years appreciate the softness and womanly strength of the other sex, maturing faster and earlier than they do, but I think that they may well experience something like the love of it, in song. They thus learn to love aright just as they should learn to dance, not because they are in love *now*, but because they *will be in love someday*.

But there is a manliness too in this love they would learn in song, a bravura, a flinging away of all things but the beloved. Here is a fine poem that Robert Burns composed for a melody in G minor, of which Napoleon said that it was the one good tune the English had:

O wert thou in the cauld blast,
On yonder lea, on yonder lea,
My plaidie to the angry airt,
I'd shelter thee, I'd shelter thee.
Or did misfortune's bitter storms
Around thee blaw, around thee blaw,

Thy shield should be my bosom,
To share it a', to share it a'.

Oh, were I in the wildest waste,
Sae black and bare, sae black and bare,
The desert were a Paradise,
If thou wert there, if thou wert there.
Or were I monarch of the globe,
With thee to reign, with thee to reign,
The brightest jewel in my crown
Wad be my queen, wad be my queen.

There is nothing specifically sexual about the poem, yet it is *all about the sexes,* all about the love of a man for a woman, regardless of circumstances. The woman makes an Eden in the wild waste merely by her being with him, and if he were the ruler of the whole world, that world would be as nothing in comparison with the sharer of his fortune, his queen. We may think of what used to be the famous lines of Edward Fitzgerald's translation of *The Rubaiyat of Omar Khayyam:*

A book of verses underneath the bough,
A jug of wine, a loaf of bread, and thou
Beside me singing in the wilderness—
That wilderness were Paradise enow!

It is well that Scripture gives to us the songbook of the ancient Hebrews, which became the songbook of the Church, near to the love song of Solomon, that song of songs. Love calls forth love. The man who cannot understand what it would mean to sing to a woman will likely not understand why anyone would sing a hymn to God: he does not have the heart for it. So let us give boys hymns to sing that train them up in a distinctly masculine form of devotion. Here is a hymn set to the Finnish melody "Suomi," a rousing cavalry march:

Lift high the triumph song today!
From Olivet to Calvary
We tread again that ancient way
Our Savior rode in majesty.
Let now the loud hosannas ring!
The Prince of Peace is passing by;
The Lord of Life, our Savior, King,
Goes bravely forth to reign and die.

Why would anyone long to walk along the ancient way of sorrow, following Christ who goes forth to his death upon Calvary? Only love can explain it, only love. This is not the love of someone who consoles you, and soothes your open wounds with balm. That is well and good and sweet, but it is not here. This is not the love of someone who is inviting you in an open embrace to take you from your world of trouble. That is well and good and filled with hope, but it is not the main thing here. Here is that masculine love of the true man whom we admire for his courage and magnificence: our hearts beat high, and if we cannot imitate him, we can at least follow where he has led before.

For that death brings life:

We open wide the gates of love!
By Olivet and Calvary,
Acclaim him Christ, from God above,
Our King, through all eternity.
Let now the loud hosannas ring!
The Prince of Peace is passing by;
The Lord of Life, our Savior, King,
Goes nobly forth, no more to die.

Can we imagine a group of boys singing that hymn? If not, again we are the oddballs. It is a hymn for all Christians, but the boys specifically will not only admire the victorious Christ, they will imagine themselves as his fellow soldiers, as they should.

So too in this famous hymn, which has been banished from most contemporary hymnals for the obvious reason that it is too lively and heartening for young men—whose heart for the faith must be dampened, lest they accomplish the very goal that the song enjoins upon them:

> *Rise up, O men of God!*
> *Have done with lesser things;*
> *Give heart and soul and mind and strength*
> *To serve the King of Kings.*
>
> *Rise up, O men of God!*
> *His kingdom tarries long;*
> *Bring in the day of brotherhood*
> *And end the night of wrong.*
>
> *Rise up, O men of God!*
> *The Church for you doth wait,*
> *Her strength unequal to her task;*
> *Rise up, and make her great!*
>
> *Lift high the cross of Christ!*
> *Tread where His feet have trod;*
> *As brothers of the Son of Man*
> *Rise up, O men of God!*

I have heard the boys of The Heights, a Catholic boys' school in Maryland, singing this song, and embodying in their voices and their high spirits the Christian manhood that the song calls forth. The song is not narcissistic. We are not urged to admire ourselves. We are not congratulating ourselves. We are not singing the words of Jesus in the first person. We are stirring ourselves to *action*. I have sung this hymn with some hundreds of seminarians at a Baptist college, in an auditorium with a rotunda, and it felt as if the walls and the roof were trembling.

A seminary is an unusual setting, I admit, and one where it is easy to imagine men singing a hymn. What about boys in a prison? When once Father Flanagan needed to raise money for additional farming acreage at Boys Town, he and a troop of boys took their show on the road, doing circus acts and singing. They were winning a lot of good will, traveling westward through Nebraska, till they came to a town where no one would give them a passing nod. The Ku Klux Klan had gotten there first, and had condemned Flanagan for teaching white boys and black boys side by side. They had also gotten to towns farther west. So Flanagan took the boys to the nearby state penitentiary, paying an unannounced call on the warden, and offering to do the show for the convicts inside. Those hardened criminals loved it and cried out for an encore. When Flanagan replied that the boys had done all the tricks they knew, the warden asked if they could sing something.

That they could. Waifs, orphans, and young delinquents released on parole to Father Flanagan sang Gounod's "Ave Maria" to five hundred convicts. Imagine the scene. And Father Flanagan determined then and there that Boys Town must have a real choir, like those he had heard when he was a seminarian in Rome and Innsbruck.

Give boys the songs. *Mos cantandi, mos amandi:* the custom of singing becomes the custom of love. We sing what we love, and we learn to love that which we sing.

From Strength to Strength Go On

On February 7, 1882, a group of boys in Cambridge, Massachusetts did something that no group of boys would now do, as it would not occur to them in a thousand years. They paid a wholly unannounced visit to the home of their favorite poet, who was celebrating his seventy-fifth birthday.

Their favorite poet?

The aged Henry Wadsworth Longfellow, who had always loved children and had had several of his own, welcomed them in most warmly, and he and the boys sat down to chat about the poems they loved, while he had his maid bring out some tea and scones. And thus did they spend that late winter afternoon.

It was the last birthday that Longfellow ever saw upon earth. He died the next month, and I doubt that any of the boys ever forgot that visit. But why would they do such a thing?

For one thing, Longfellow had always had a heart for them, and so they had a heart for him. Here is a stanza from "My Lost Youth," a poem from which Robert Frost would take the title for *A Boy's Will*, his own first book of verses. The poet is going back in his memory to the seaside town where he grew up:

> *I remember the bulwarks by the shore,*
> *And the fort upon the hill;*
> *The sunrise gun, with its hollow roar,*
> *The drum-beat repeated o'er and o'er,*
> *And the bugle wild and shrill.*
> *And the music of that old song*
> *Throbs in my memory still:*
> *"A boy's will is the wind's will,*
> *And the thoughts of youth are long, long thoughts."*

Each stanza ends with those two lines, the final one all the more powerful for not being rhymed. Longfellow took that one straight from an old Lapland song. We may well assume that when Lapland men thought of their own youth, they had no political aims in mind. There were no cities in the land of the reindeer and the midnight sun and months of twilight and darkness. They were thinking of the boy, the essential youth, whose thoughts are—or used to be, before the short circuiting of the brain, and school—"long, long thoughts," like thoughts of voyages, or treks across the wilderness, far away. There is no telling where the wind or the boy's will may go.

It is well that Longfellow took that line from a people for whom writing came very late, because it reminds us that poetry is the one art that every culture but our own has not only partaken of but has had at its center, poetry and song. Those were not for girls and effeminate boys. I am reminded of a famous scene recounted by Saint Bede the Venerable in his *Ecclesiastical History of the English People.* It was evening at the monastery of Whitby, and a group of illiterate herdsmen and farm workers were in one of the outbuildings enjoying a *gebeorscip*, that is, a party with beer. We must think of burly Germanic men, probably smelling strong of animals and hay, hungry and thirsty, and eager for some innocent pleasure.

When I used to ask my college students what important thing was yet missing from this scene, they usually replied, "Women!" But that was not it. What the Germans wanted was music. So a harp—some kind of stringed instrument that you plucked and strummed—went around the table, and when it came to you, it was your turn to sing a song. Please keep in mind that not one of those men could read or write. They sang real poetry, such as the *scop* or singer did at Hrothgar's hall in *Beowulf*: singing of the brave deeds of heroes and gods of old. One of their number, Caedmon, left the party before the harp came to him, because he was ashamed; he claimed he did not know any songs to sing. It's hard to hold up your head among German men when you don't know your heroic poetry.

An interesting thing then happened to Caedmon, involving a dream, an angel, a short and brilliant hymn composed in his sleep, a visit on the morrow to the abbess, a test run to see if he could turn a story from Scripture—read to him, of course, because he could not read—into a song by the next day, and then his enthusiastic welcome as a monk in the monastery, followed by a life of composing, not writing but composing, songs based upon Scripture and the lives of the saints in the same meter that the Germans had used for centuries for their heroic verse.

That is the heritage of mankind, such poetry, and men and boys were always at the heart of it. From it they learned high and noble aspirations, the beauty of the courageous deed, and honor and fidelity and steadfastness, and when Europe was made Europe by the Christian faith, they learned chivalry too, the meek and gentlemanly answer even in the heat of battle. So we find that poignant moment near the climax of *The Song of Roland*, when the two noble friends, Roland and Oliver, each one near death, forgive one another. For they were in the rear guard of Charlemagne's army as it was crossing through the dangerous passes of the Pyrenees from Muslim-controlled Spain into France. They were thus ambushed on all sides by the Muslims, betrayed by Ganelon, stepfather of Roland, who hated him intensely. When Oliver pleaded with Roland to sound the Olliphant, his horn, to call to Charlemagne for assistance, Roland refused, partly for pride and partly to protect Charlemagne. That made for hard words between them, with Oliver accusing him of foolishness. The rear guard is massacred. But Roland and Oliver continue to fight. Oliver, so badly wounded that he can no longer see, has given Roland a blow unwittingly. Roland turns to him in gentleness and friendship. Thus will they go to their deaths as brothers, reconciled:

> At such a blow Roland regards him keen,
> And asks of him, in gentle tones and sweet,
> "To do this thing, my comrade, did you mean?
> This is Roland, who ever held you dear,

And no mistrust was ever us between."
Says Oliver: "Now I can hear you speak;
I struck you now: and for your pardon plead."
Answers Roland: "I am not hurt, indeed;
I pardon you, before God's throne and here."

And each man bows to the other. No action could better capture their manly respect and the more than manly acknowledgment of wrong, with complete forgiveness, in but a few words and one simple gesture. But that is all that is needed.

Our boys should be in the tent with Achilles and the aged King Priam, who has come to beg for the body of his beloved son Hector, and Achilles, as stern and inflexible as death, finally gives up his anger and enters the human race again. They should be riding with Paul Revere, in Longfellow's poem, warning the minutemen that the British were coming. They should ride into the valley of death with the six hundred at Balaclava. They should walk the wall between Robert Frost and his neighbor, and sail the seas with the ancient Mariner and his heavy guilt, and hear with Coleridge the Ethiopian maiden singing of Mount Abora.

"Lift up your hearts," says the priest at Mass. And why should boys not do that every day of their lives?

Enemies to Slay

The Gospels of Matthew and Luke place the birth of Jesus in the midst of danger, not simply to the child, but to those whom the child will bring down. In Matthew, we hear that Herod, that potent and bloodthirsty pretender to the Jewish faith, tries to ascertain through the Magi who and where the child is, that he also may come and adore him, the true king of the Jews. When his plan fails, he tries to make sure of his position by ordering the massacre of every boy born in or near Bethlehem in the previous two years. Nicola Pisano sculpted the scene for one of the eight panels of his pulpit in the cathedral of Siena, which he worked on in the years 1265 to 1268. In that panel, the long-bearded Herod sits atop the fray, gesturing downward, while beneath him the slaughter goes on. The soldiers are bearded also, with low brows, and in the crowded and chaotic scene, they appear to be enjoying themselves in a ferociously stupid way, while the women look on, wailing, and their little boys are stabbed in their sight. Not one man is in the scene to protect them. It is mother and child, but no Joseph. The only men are murderers. So were the words of the prophet fulfilled: "In Rama there was a voice heard, lamentation, and weeping, and great mourning, Rachel weeping for her children, and would not be comforted, because they are not" (Mt 2:18; cf. Jer 31:15 KJV).

151

In Luke, who recounts an earlier incident, we hear that Joseph and Mary bring Jesus to the Temple to be consecrated to the Lord. And in the Temple, there was an old man named Simeon, whom God had promised that he would not die until he had seen the Messiah, the Anointed of the Lord. When Simeon saw the baby Jesus, he took him in his arms and blessed God in a canticle of gratitude and praise, and then he turned to Mary and Joseph, and said, "Behold, this child is set for the fall and rising again of many in Israel; and a sign which shall be spoken against; (Yea, a sword shall pierce through thy own soul also,) that the thoughts of many hearts may be revealed" (Lk 2:34–35 KJV). Andrea Mantegna (ca. 1465) has painted the scene with frank dramatic power. We see it through an open window, with Mary's elbow placed on and outside of the sill, intruding into our "space," so that we feel that we are there, hearing the words that the painting implies but cannot speak. Mary and Simeon face one another, Mary holding the child still in swaddling bands and crying, as if Jesus also understood the prophecy of suffering that he must fulfill. Mary looks earnestly at the old man, and Mantegna has painted her as if she were a sturdy Italian peasant woman, with a strong protective spirit in her. Between her and Simeon, in the near background, stands Joseph, glaring, with his jaw set. He too has heard the words, and he looks as if the enemy were gaining upon them already, and challenging him to fight.

Jesus, grown to manhood, combines in his person and his preaching the ideal of the suffering servant, who did not return violence for violence but was "brought as a lamb to the slaughter, and as a sheep before her shearers is dumb, so he openeth not his mouth" (Is 53:7 KJV), and the ideal of the fighter and conqueror, who "must reign, till he hath put all enemies under his feet," as Saint Paul says, and "the last enemy that shall be destroyed is death" (1 Cor 15:25–26 KJV). For this life of ours is for wayfaring and warfaring, not separate from one another or against one another, but shoulder to shoulder against the enemy of man. Therefore Saint Paul advises the Christians at Ephesus to be fully armed infantrymen in the army of God "that ye may stand against the wiles of the devil. For we wrestle not against flesh and blood, but against principalities, against powers, against the rulers of the darkness of this world, against spiritual wickedness in high places" (Eph 6:11–12 KJV).

This determination to fight is not for personal vengeance against someone who has done us wrong. In that case, Jesus commands us to turn the other cheek (see Mt 5:39). It is a form of love for our neighbor, and of zealous love for God. It sounds in thrilling tones in the words of Jesus when the disciples he sent forth to preach and heal have come back triumphant: "I beheld Satan as lightning fall from heaven" (Lk 10:18 KJV). It resounds in the final words of Saint Paul to his disciple Timothy: "I have fought a good fight, I have finished my course, I have kept the faith" (2 Tm 4:7 KJV). It shines with terrible and cleansing light in the figure of the Son, revealed to the meek and elderly John on Patmos, as him from whose mouth came a sharp double-edged sword (see Rv 1:16), and who will, after the final and utter defeat of Satan and his swarming evils, "give to every man according as his work shall be" (22:12 KJV).

We may suppose that in this world, which God has made to be one of real adventure, where good lies on the far side of danger, even the danger of love, the ideal of the fighter will always shine out brightly. It is so beyond this world also. For God is revealed to us in Scripture as the God *of hosts,* that is, of armies, the heavenly armies of angels hierarchically organized, seraphim and cherubim, thrones, dominions, virtues, princedoms, powers, archangels, and angels. They were so before the fall of Satan, or we may think of them as being so regardless of the fall of Satan if we suppose that that fall was instantaneous. The soldier fights *for,* more than he fights *against.* He has enemies to slay only because he has, first of all, a master to serve, friends to hearten, a country to defend, and a family to protect. The true soldier is a man of love.

So John Ruskin, in *Unto This Last* (1860), says that soldiers have always been held in higher esteem than men of trade, and this is only right and just:

> For the soldier's trade, verily and essentially, is not slaying, but being slain. This, without well knowing its own meaning, the world honours it for. A bravo's trade is slaying; but the world has never respected bravos more than merchants: the reason it honours the soldier is, because he holds his life at the service of the State. Reckless he may be—fond of pleasure or of adventure—all kinds of bye-motives and mean impulses may have determined the choice of his profession, and may affect (to all appearance exclusively) his daily conduct in it; but our estimate of him is based on this ultimate fact—of which we are well assured—that, put him in a fortress breach, with all the pleasures of the world behind him, and only death and his duty in front of him, he will keep his face to the front; and he knows that this choice may be put to him at any moment, and has beforehand taken his part—virtually takes such part continually—does, in reality, die daily.

And so we must teach our boys to be, whether they are soldiers in fact or no. Ruskin did not want to make his readers into soldiers enlisting in the British army and navy. He wanted instead to imbue laborers, artisans, and merchants with the ideal of the soldier so that they too might give of themselves so fully, and especially in times of national trouble. Just as the soldier must lay his life on the line for the sake of his fellows, so the artisan should subordinate all considerations of mere gain, however important they may be, to the quality of his work, and so the merchant should gain honor by refraining from taking advantage of the distress of others, but should instead think of himself as duty-bound to provide goods to his countrymen. Thus it is that Ruskin did not justify the soldier by saying that he made merchants possible, but justified the merchant by urging him to become more like the loyal and life-giving soldier.

Salvation From the Unexpected

It is night, off an island in the Caribbean. A boy is on the sea, in a coracle, a roundish little boat that takes some skill to paddle, lest you just go round in circles. He has no experience with such a boat. Neither his friends nor his enemies know where he is, and if he should float off too far from the island, his friends will think that he had abandoned them and been lost, and his enemies will shrug and spit and think no more of it. There is a real chance that that will happen. He is trying to intercept the ship floating off shore, which is now in the hands of a couple of mutineers. His idea is to cut the anchor off in secret and have the ship float toward the island with the tide, frustrating the plans of the enemy. He is counting on the two men being inattentive and drunk, or dead, having killed one another. He makes his slow way toward the ship, and takes hold of the rope: "The hawser was taut as a bowstring and the current so strong that she pulled upon her anchor. All round the hull, in the blackness, the rippling current bubbled and chattered like a little mountain stream. One cut with my sea gully, and the *Hispaniola* would go humming down the tide."

He thinks: if he cuts the rope while there is such strain on it, the ship will buck suddenly like a horse and he will likely be flung to his death. So he waits till the wind changes and the ship moves into the current, loosening the hawser. At that point, he takes out his knife, opens it with his teeth, and cuts the hawser down to a couple of mere strands. The ship shifts again, and the boy must wait before he severs the hawser completely. In the meantime, he overhears the men aboard, swearing and fighting. An empty bottle is thrown out of the cabin window. When at last he cuts the hawser, the ship veers straight against him, and in a moment of decision he grabs hold of a stray rope hanging over the side and pulls himself up to look into the cabin. There he sees a fight to the death, and that will determine the next fateful decision he will make. For when the ship, many hours later, turns and threatens to run the coracle down, the boy will board it himself and take possession of it, he, Jim Hawkins, compelled to employ the skill and the cunning of the surviving devil on board, Israel Hands.

The reader may recognize the novel: *Treasure Island* by Robert Louis Stevenson, and the boy-hero Jim Hawkins. He may recall too that once the ship is safely in harbor, Hands will try to kill the boy, who escapes from him by climbing the mizzen-shrouds and sitting on the crosstrees, with pistols drawn. "One more step, Mr. Hands," Jim says, "and I'll blow your brains out! Dead men don't bite, you know," he says, chuckling, tossing Hands' own words back in his teeth. Hands pretends to give in, but with a sudden sling of his arm, he throws his dagger at the boy, pinning his shoulder to the mast. The pistols go off, and Hands plunges to his death beneath.

Jim Hawkins does not have superpowers. He does not whirl like a dervish to deliver a punch with a small fist or a kick with a small foot to send men twice his size sprawling, as do choreo-graphed women in the silliest of our action-movies. He does not presume to lead the good Squire Trelawney or Doctor Livesey or Captain Smollett. The novel is fantastic, and yet realistic. Jim does only what a boy might do, and what only a boy with con-siderable pluck would do, especially since for much of the book he does not have either the protection or the understanding of the men he loves and defends. For a while, they even believe that he has joined the mutineers—to save his skin and to be with those of greater numbers. So the doctor finds him with the bad men after he has, unbeknownst to both friend and enemy, saved the Hispaniola and hidden her in a cove around the other side of the island: "'So, Jim,' said the doctor, sadly, 'here you are. As you have brewed, so shall you drink, my boy. Heaven knows I cannot find it in my heart to blame you; but this much I will say, be it kind or unkind: when Captain Smollett was well you dared not have gone off, and when he was ill, and couldn't help it, by George, it was downright cowardly!'"

The real courage requires doing what is good and right even when you will get no credit for it, certainly not from your enemies, but not even from your friends. At this point, Jim breaks down and tells the doctor what he has done to save the ship, and why he is where he is. The doctor is a man of quick understanding and just judgment. "Every step it's you that save our lives," he says.

It will not do to say that Jim Hawkins is a "stereotype." He is a boy, through and through, *and that is why he appeals to us,* immediately and powerfully. When we read about his adventure, we do not say, "A boy would never do that." We say, "I wish I were that boy!" Since that is so, what is our excuse for not giving boys such stories to nourish them?

The few good men from the *Hispaniola* are saved by a boy, not because the boy is a genius or a Goliath, but because he is self-reliant, stubborn, plucky, shrewd, and *self-sacrificing.* When we say that salvation comes to us whence we least expect it, we imply that courage is best shown when you remain loyal to what appears to be a lost cause, when you are outnumbered, when the enemy is confident, and your friends waver, or doubt you, or abandon you. It is not that you are "an army of one," which is a self-contradiction. It is that you conform yourself to the pattern of Christ himself.

Here the boy must stand against the pull of the social. It is comfortable to be in a crowd, and when the crowd roars, it is but a many-headed bully, unreasoning and without direction, unless by the demonic. The first enemy to be put down then is the enemy within, the sweet-talking one, the one that would have you raise your weapon *only* in the safety of others doing the same, and never against those who would be your friends, false friends but comfortable ones, if you would only do what they are doing, and not trouble them with contradiction.

So in *Paradise Lost* was the angel Abdiel, whose name means "Servant of God," when Satan first assembled his underlings in rebellion in heaven against the Most High. After Satan mocks Abdiel in sight of all the others, and refuses to listen to reason and to warnings, Abdiel has these words to say:

> *"That golden scepter which thou didst reject*
> *Is now an iron rod to bruise and break*
> *Thy disobedience. Well thou didst advise,*
> *Yet not for thy advise or threats I fly*
> *These wicked Tents devoted, lest the wrath*
> *Impendent, raging into sudden flame*
> *Distinguish not: for soon expect to feel*
> *His Thunder on thy head, devouring fire.*
> *Then who created thee lamenting learn,*
> *When who can uncreate thee thou shalt know."*
> *So spake the Seraph Abdiel faithful found,*
> *Among the faithless, faithful only he;*
> *Among innumerable false, unmoved,*
> *Unshaken, unseduced, unterrified*
> *His loyalty he kept, his love, his zeal;*
> *Nor number, nor example with him wrought*
> *To swerve from truth, or change his constant mind*
> *Though single. From amidst them forth he passed,*

Long way through hostile scorn, which he sustained
Superior, nor of violence feared aught;
And with retorted scorn his back he turned
On those proud towers to swift destruction doomed.

Jim Hawkins will be returned to the true men, and Abdiel will make his way to the rest of the angels who have remained loyal to God, and his will be the honor of the first blow struck against Satan, one that lands so hard upon his crest that the apostate angel must retreat ten paces, and is forced against his will to bend the knee to the ground, as if in the attitude of adoration that he has rejected.

We see here that to fight will require sometimes being alone, and that is a hard thing for any person to be, much less a mere boy. And so? It still does not mean that you go along and shrug, as if the fight were useless. Nor does it mean that you will remain alone, because the army of the good *does* stand behind you, even if you do not see them, and there will come a time, even if it is only in the eternal presence of God, when you will join their ranks again. So Abdiel hears from God himself:

Servant of God, well done, well hast thou fought
The better fight, who single hast maintained
Against revolted multitudes the Cause
Of Truth, in word mightier than they in arms;
And for the testimony of Truth hast borne
Universal reproach, far worse to bear
Than violence: for this was all thy care
To stand approved in sight of God, though Worlds
Judged thee perverse: the easier conquest now
Remains thee, aided by this host of friends,
Back on thy foes more glorious to return
Than scorned thou didst depart.

"Well done, good and faithful servant!" says the rich man in Jesus' parable. "Enter into the joy of thy Master."

What stories do we give our boys to learn from? Here is Father Eligius Weir discussing the mental malformation of a certain young man who had graduated from delinquency to murder: "He lived in phantasy the parts of 'hard-boiled guys' who hero'd the 10 and 15 cent novels that littered his room." Then the young man got from an episode of Gangbusters the idea and the go-ahead to use a pistol he had procured to kill one of his rivals, a boy who worked at his family's delicatessen. The words of Father Weir seem almost quaint to our modern ears, as those dreadful little novels might appear relatively naive and innocent, by comparison with what a boy can pick up on line, or from his school library.

A Heart for Praise

"He did not know how to retreat," said the Protestant editor of *The Christian Herald* on the occasion of the death of Father Flanagan of Boys Town. "He was on the march, and when last seen by mortal eyes, he, too, was going forward." He has gone now, says the minister, "to his coronation." The same Father Flanagan said that most boys want to do what is right, because they want to *be praised*. This desire warrants some careful thought.

The scene is a castle, governed by the lady Alma. Two knights errant have arrived, and after assisting the castle guards against an attack by their enemies from without, they have been welcomed in for supper. The lords and ladies arrange themselves around a great table, and one of the knights, Prince Arthur—who will one day be King Arthur—is seated next to a lovely lady who looks pensive and sad. When Arthur asks her why she should be so, she replies that she is just what he is, since he has been wandering through all England searching for the woman of whom he has dreamed, the Faerie Queen, and has not found her yet. She too is pensive "for great desire of glory and of fame." Arthur blushes with self-consciousness, and asks his companions at the table who the lady is. Her name, they tell him, is Praise-Desire, "that by well doing sought to honor to aspire" (*The Faerie Queene*, II.ix.38.7). She is pointedly *not*, as the poet Edmund Spenser implicitly shows us, that daughter of the money-god and power-broker Mammon, whom we have met in his caverns and gold foundry under the earth. Mammon's daughter is named Philotime, for honor wrongly lusted after: alternatively, *Ambition.*

The proud man wants to put himself on display, as an idol for others to gaze upon. He wants the praise or the flattery or the obeisance of those he seeks to keep beneath him. The suitors to Ambition in the cave of Mammon do not care for right doing, but for high rank regardless of how they come by it:

> *Those that were up themselves, kept others low,*
> *Those that were low themselves, held others hard,*
> *Ne suffered them to rise or greater grow,*
> *But every one did strive his fellow down to throw.* (II. vii.47.6-9)

It is as if they were, in their souls, the lowest of the low— professors at an academic meeting at a modern university, jockeying for position, and fighting with all the greater ferocity because no one outside of their circle even knows who they are.

But to desire praise aright, for any human being, is to acknowledge in some respect the *superiority* of those who confer the praise, and to accept that praise not as payment due but as an act of appreciative love. Praise is the grateful gift of man to God in return for all the graces that God confers, including existence itself, and praise of man by God is his way of welcoming man into his life and his joy. Boys seek praise not for their beauty but for what they have done, and not from those who praise them *because* they love them but from those who they believe have justly prized their deeds. The praise that comes from such a man is itself an act of disinterested love.

Such a healthy desire for praise is not the same as toadying or apple polishing. Boys naturally despise that sort of thing. That is a bribe, posing as affection. Again, think of sports, not beauty contests. You are safe or out at the plate regardless of the affection of your mother in the stands, or the wishes of the umpire. When the boy hears his father say, "Son, you lost half a stride when you ran straight on to third base and then had to turn, rather than rounding the bag like so," he knows that the father is acting as a disinterested judge, and he will—if the judgments are sound and not surly—take it as a compliment to his maturity. When after the next game he hears the old man say, "Son, you rounded that bag this time just right, and it's lucky for your team that you did it. Way to go," he will flush with the feeling of things well done, and will likely remember that moment for the rest of his life. Never underestimate the power of a father's praise. "He picks blueberries like an old-timer," said my father to another man, in my presence, when I was only a small boy. "He picks them clean, and he doesn't talk." That moment takes *second* place in my memory to the time when my father wrote to me, thirteen years later, to say that I was the smartest person he ever knew in his life. Deeds count.

I think here of a moment in John Ford's loving tribute to West Point, *The Long Gray Line*. The situation is one to wring the heart. The elderly Sergeant Martin Maher and his wife, Mary, have lived as a couple on the grounds of the academy all their married lives. They have seen class after class of young men come and go. Martin and Mary have no children of their own. Their only son died at birth, and Mary could never bear a child again. So they have adopted the boys of West Point and taken them to their hearts. Most especially they have loved Martin's godson, "Red" Sundstrom, whose father, also "Red," died in the very last action of World War One. Junior follows in his father's steps and enrolls at West Point, but just before graduation, he breaks the cadet's code of honor by contracting a marriage to his girlfriend and going on a four-day honeymoon. The act was one of impulse. Red and his girl regretted it immediately, and had the marriage annulled. Nobody knows about it at the school. But Red has to tell someone. He opens his heart to old Martin, hoping against hope that Martin will let him off the hook. Martin tells the young man that he will not expose him, but that he broke his oath, and he knows what the right thing to do is. He must turn himself in. Martin says it, even in the face of Mary's impassioned cry, that if he does this thing to Red, she will never forgive him.

Red makes the decision himself, renouncing his commission and entering the regular Army as a private, ready to fight in World War Two. He shakes Martin's hand and bids him and Mary goodbye. It is all right.

It is a few years later. Mary has passed away. Martin is alone at home on Christmas Eve when several of the cadets show up to cook a meal for him, decorate his Christmas tree, and ask him to rank the best football players for Army that he has seen. Then comes a knock on the door.

"Big brass," says one of the boys to Martin. "Really big brass." A hush comes to all.

Martin enters the parlor, and there stands no general, no superintendent, but the enlisted man Red, walking with a cane. He has fought bravely and well, and made not only sergeant major, the highest rank for an enlisted man, but has earned his captain's stripes for his courage and intelligence on the field. His brown coat is decked out in medals. The cadets look upon him with admiration and deference.

Red holds out to Martin the greatest medal of all, the Congressional Medal of Honor. "I wanted *you* to pin it on me, Marty," he says. The boy, boy no more but true man, asks the better man, not the better soldier in the field but the better man, to give him that official recognition of his honorable deeds.

The Kingdom of Heaven Suffers Violence

Love is swift of foot;
Love's a man of war,
  And can shoot,
And hit from far.

From George Herbert, "Discipline"

"The Lord is a man of war," sings Moses on the safe side of the waters, "Pharaoh's chariots and his hosts he hath cast into the sea" (Ex 15:3–4 KJV). The poet Herbert understood that God is both a man of war and that he is Love, as says Saint John, and if that is so, then we should not suppose that the one is in contradiction with the other. It is *because* God is Love that he is the man of war. Hirelings allow the wolves to enter the fold and to devour the sheep. Wicked priests in our own time have used boys as objects of sick and effeminate pleasure. Wicked bishops have permitted it. But the Lord, our Shepherd, smites the enemy. He guides us and guards us through the valley of the shadow of death. "Thy rod and thy staff," says the psalmist, "they comfort me." They give him strength. They are not crutches. They are for bloodying the head of the ravenous wolf.

Let boys then know without apology that he who fights best for what is right loves best. God himself "trains my fingers to fight," says the psalmist, and from Jesus himself we derive the mysterious verse that inspired Dante with rapture before the wonders of divine grace. Says the Eagle of Justice, explaining to the pilgrim poet how it is that two men, apparently pagan, Ripheus the Trojan and the Roman emperor Trajan, are among the most exalted souls in the sphere of Jupiter, that of the Just Rulers:

> *The kingdom of heaven suffers violence*
> > *from living hope and burning charity,*
> > *that overcome the will of the divine,*
> *Not as a man will overcome a man—*
> > *the divine wins because it would be won,*
> > *and won, it wins with its benignity.*

The violence of fervent love, says the Eagle, has made way for these men who no one would expect to be in heaven. Pope Gregory the Great, the legend went, so ardently admired the virtue of Trajan, and prayed for him so assiduously, that the emperor, more than four centuries after his death, was resuscitated and so could hear the word of God. And he in turn fell in love, and thus merited his entry into paradise.

God rewards the ardent, not the tepid. The angel of the Lord wrestled with Jacob and then gave him the new name Israel to commemorate the encounter, the struggle. God led Abraham to dare to turn his will when he revealed his condemnation of the evil cities of the plain, and Abraham finally won from God the agreement that Sodom and Gomorrah would be spared if there were but ten just men to be found therein. Jesus tells us to knock on the door of God, and in one of his parables, the obstreperous neighbor continues to knock until his friend, already in bed and with his children settled and not wanting to move, gets up and answers his need. God wants sons and not slaves, as we learn from Saint Paul. Slaves do not fight for their masters, or they fight with half a heart and a slow hand, but sons, true sons fight with a will on behalf of their fathers and those whom their fathers love.

But that implies also that the son should be willing to accept love in the form of discipline—which is the title of the poem I have cited above. The *disciple* is literally the pupil, the learner: Greek *mathetes*. We can learn lessons in history and geography by study. We do not learn any lessons at all in life without discipline: which implies love, for "whom best I love, I cross," says Jupiter in Shakespeare's *Cymbeline*, for "whom the Lord loveth he chasteneth, and scourgeth every son whom he receiveth" (Heb 12:6 KJV). The verse applies to human beings regardless of sex, and yet we may see in it a special appeal specifically to sons, and a wise and loving regard for their weakness. God knows our frailty, and will not try us beyond our capacity to endure. He knows our frailty, and therefore he tries us at times within our capacity to endure it, that we might not be frail always. "Strengthen your brothers," says Jesus to Saint Peter (see Lk 22:32). "We rejoice in our sufferings," says Saint Paul, "knowing that suffering produces endurance, and endurance produces character, and character produces hope, and hope does not disappoint us, because God's love has been poured into our hearts" (Rom 5:3–6).

There is a real joy in the fight. We are not talking about the grim and suicidal, or the grim and murderous. Here are the words of a true Christian warrior, a lover of poetry, of the woman he married and to whom he is writing, and of his country. He is Sergeant Joyce Kilmer, writing home from the front in France, in the First World War. "Dangers shared together and hardships mutually borne," he says, "develops in us a sort of friendship I never knew in civilian life, a friendship clean of jealousy and gossip and envy and suspicion—a fine hearty roaring mirthful sort of thing, like an open fire of whole pine-trees in a giant's castle" (May 24, 1918). This to the woman he loved so dearly that in the same letter he says his love and his memory bind him so strongly they cut like cords into his flesh, but he is confident that he and she, no matter what happens in the battlefield, will be one together for eternity.

Fighting, for boys—not on their own behalf, selfishly, but for those they love, in acts of self-giving courage—is invigorating. It is, dare we say, *fun.* "The female of the species is more deadly than the male," wrote Kipling, thinking of what she will do with tooth and claw to protect her young. With men—with boys—it is or it can be something other than that, other than that blessed ferocity. Let me illustrate. Again I turn to Richard Llewellyn's autobiographical novel *How Green Was My Valley.* When the young Huw Morgan is sent to the village several miles off, walking there and back each day, he encounters a young English teacher who has nothing but scorn for the dirty "guttersnipes" of Cwm Rhondda, the coal mining vale where the Morgans live. One of the bigger boys in the class, when school is out, takes up the train of contempt, and, with an assist from a fellow, beats Huw to a bloody mess.

When Huw comes home, his father does not ask him how he feels. He knows how the boy feels. He asks him if he has *won.* He has not. Then he asks him if he wants to continue at the school. He does. That settles it: the father begins to teach Huw the gentlemanly art of fisticuffs, much to Mrs. Morgan's trepidation. When the bully tries to pummel Huw the next time, *he learns better* too, as Huw weaves and dodges and ducks, and lands blow after blow. The result of the fight is *not* that the two boys become bitter enemies. It is the reverse: they gain real respect for one another. They have now both given and taken punches. They understand, too, that Huw has not fought simply for himself. He has fought for Cwm Rhondda and for his father and mother and sisters and brothers. He has fought for their honor.

They are like men on a battlefield who, having done their best in the cause of their country, and having left it to God to sort out the ultimate disposition of the war, die on the field together and awake to clear their heads and shake hands, and smile rather sheepishly, yet with delight. The ideological pacifist is by comparison a pinched little soul. Or if we notice, and rightly, that war is filled with all the evils that men would avoid, we might conclude that sometimes, in the hearts of strong Christian men, love alone would be sufficient for them to storm those gates of hell; love alone endures the discipline; love alone tells us why a man would lay down his life for his friends. So the poet Torquato Tasso imagines Godfrey of Bouillon, the ultimate leader of the first band of crusaders in their conquest of Jerusalem, as a man of love, not hate. God looks down upon the chiefs with his sight that "spies into the heart / of human loves in deepest secrecy," and sees "Godfrey ardent for one aim, to rout / the heathen from the land of the Most High." It is the warmth and the right ordering of love that God desires from his fighters. He is not nice, but holy; not tame, but good: the ultimate good.

It will not do to pretend that boys are going to be other than what they are. It is nature crying out, in the blood and the bones. You will make them into good men, or you will let them lapse and become bad men, or frustrated, inept, selfish, resentful non-men; you will not make them into women. Burn that fact into the mind. You can make them into valiant fighters for the right, or you can let them err and grow wicked; or you can force upon them an unnatural confinement, breaking their spirits, as you would hobble a horse you mean only for a treadmill, and then glue. You cannot make women out of them. You would be mad and cruel to try. It would be no act of love or discipline. It would be an act of the madness of ideology, or sheer cold selfishness.

The Noble Opponent

Joseph Cannon, possibly the most powerful speaker of the House in American history, once said of Theodore Roosevelt that he had no more use for the Constitution than a tomcat had of a marriage license. Cannon and Roosevelt belonged to the *same party,* but Cannon was one of the conservative old guard, while Roosevelt was a progressive. They were enemies, yet many was the time when Cannon visited the president in the White House, and they got things done.

When William Sherman died, Joseph E. Johnston, a former general for the Confederate Army, and the man whom Sherman out-maneuvered and defeated in his brutal march from Atlanta to Savannah and the sea, traveled to New York City to be a pallbearer at the funeral. Sherman and Johnston admired one another, and with reason. They had hammered out an agreement at Bennett Place, in North Carolina, that ended in the surrender, on humane and generous terms, of ninety thousand Confederate soldiers. Sherman told the men they could keep their side-arms and their horses, and could go home, back to work. He suffered much vituperation for it from the radical Union press and from those Republicans in the Congress who dig and grind their fists into the defeated South. Johnston never forgot the grace of his old nemesis, and he and Sherman became good friends. On that rainy day in New York, General Johnston refused to wear a hat, because, as he said, if he were in the coffin and Sherman were helping to carry it, he would not keep his head covered either. Johnston caught pneumonia from the exposure on that day, and died soon after.

John Adams and Thomas Jefferson were close friends during the American Revolution, but it was inevitable that they would clash. Adams leaned toward the British, and was deeply suspicious of the French Revolution, which Jefferson supported heartily. Adams was shrewd, often gloomy, hard-bitten, and not a man to win the love of the people. Jefferson was dashing, brilliant, and sometimes possessed of a shocking naivete, as when he said that it would be a good thing for a nation to discard all of its laws every generation or so. Adams is remembered as a failed president, defeated by his former friend in 1800. Jefferson won his two terms and, with the Louisiana Purchase, doubled the size of the United States at a catch of the breath. Their antagonism was indeed personal, not just political, and for many years they might as well have lived on the opposite sides of a vast glacial sea. Yet when Jefferson retired from the presidency, and both men grew older and mellower, they renewed their old friendship by a copious and remarkable habit of correspondence. "Thomas Jefferson survives," said Adams, with resignation, on the day of his death, July 4, 1826, the fiftieth anniversary of the Declaration of Independence. But Jefferson himself had already died that morning in Virginia.

Basketball players Larry Bird and Magic Johnson fought one another for years on the court, with Bird doing more than his share of trash-talking. In an eight-year stretch, Bird's Celtics won three championships and Johnson's Lakers won four; they faced each other in the finals three times, with the Lakers winning two. Nobody ever thought that Bird was the more stylish player, or faster, or stronger than his titanic opponent, but Johnson himself said that when Bird was determined, no human being on the court could stop him.

In the comical late western *McLintock!*, G. W. McLintock (John Wayne) reminisces with his old friend and old enemy, the Indian chief Puma. McLintock still wears a big scar from one of their battles of yore, from an arrow that nearly killed him. Now Puma comes to "Big McLintock" to beg him to appeal on behalf of the Indians to the territorial government. The braves want to live like men, he says, not women. They do not want to be fed and housed and clothed. They want to kill their own food. They have no more claims upon the land; they only want the freedom of the wilderness. McLintock does more than plead their case. He makes sure that a large cache of rifles and ammunition are put into their possession.

Boys understand the phenomenon: the worthy opponent, the one who makes you better than you were before, the one to whom it is no shame to lose, and whom it is glorious but also chastening to defeat. It is the mighty wrestling match between the brash young king Gilgamesh and the man from the wilds, Enkidu, sent by the gods to tame Gilgamesh;s arrogant heart. When Gilgamesh one night steps out into the square of his city, Uruk, to demand the first rights to another man's bride, Enkidu plants his leg against him to block his way. And the two fought like giant bulls, and, says the ancient poet, "the walls shook"— and there is no city without walls to protect the grain from marauders. Gilgamesh *should* be warlike, but he should also be a shepherd to the people, not their persecutor. The only thing that can win him to true humanity is the "match" against the man who will be his dearest friend, his "little brother," Enkidu. Their first encounter is a fight that sets in the balance the very possibility of civilization. When Gilgamesh throws his opponent, having taxed his strength to the utmost, he gives up his arrogance, and Enkidu honors his superior. From that point on, we hear no more of Gilgamesh's stealing other men's brides or conscripting young men for never-ending wars. On the contrary, the two fast friends then go forth together into the dark woods of the north to defeat—*together*—the wild god of the cedars, Humbaba, much to the enrichment and beautification of Uruk.

Lands to Tame

The worthy enemy is also the land, the sea, and all the stubborn particularities of a world that resists man's will. "Thorns also and thistles shall it bring forth to thee," says God to Adam when he sends him out of Eden into the wide world (Gn 3:18 KJV). The boy with a man's heart welcomes the challenge. He is like Louis Agassiz exploring the glaciers of western Canada, having a colleague lower him hundreds of feet into a crevasse so that he could take measurements of the ice. He is like, to bring things closer to the ordinary family, Charles Ingalls, the restless father of Laura Ingalls Wilder, who would no sooner carve a farm out of the woods of Wisconsin than he would long to go farther west, to take upon himself the taming of new land, living in a home literally dug out of a bank of earth, or in an old shack built by the railroad men along a line going west from the Dakotas.

Alexander the Great, military genius and irrepressible marauder, might have gone on conquering and building cities he named Alexandria all the way to the Pacific Ocean had not his men threatened to mutiny, and so he turned back from the Indus River and the Punjab. But Plutarch says that when he heard a philosopher discoursing about other worlds than this, Alexander wept, because he had been limited only to one. I do not praise the form that this battle-longing took in Alexander, or Genghis Khan, or Timur the Lame, the self-styled "Scourge of God," but I take note of that battle-longing and say that without it, we would have nothing of the world we so easily take for granted. Who was the first man to fell a tall tree, and burn out its innards, and caulk its sides with pitch, and float it on the water? Who first had that picture in his mind, and who, despite all the obvious difficulties, managed not only to dwell upon the picture, but to allow it to move him to long, arduous, and dangerous action? What man's hand first bound a sharp stone to a stock, and swung it at a tree trunk? Or what man's hand first dug the rich ore out of the earth, and built a roaring fire in an oven, forcing air to make it burn the hotter, so that the heat would melt the good strong ore and separate it from the dross?

Danger everywhere, and seemingly impossible tasks. There are great fish out on the sea, rich for food, but how do you get them? Grasses with good rich kernels grow wild along the flats near the Nile. How shall we grow them in vast fields all the way up and down the banks of the great river? A tremendous and unknown force sends lightning bolts from the atmosphere to the earth, and where they strike, they melt and burn and reduce to ash. How might we harness that electric power? We hear the famous account of Benjamin Franklin flying a kite in an electric storm, at the end of the kite a metal key to attract the power. The boy in him flies that kite. Young Tom Edison won a chance to work in a telegraph office when he saved the boss's small son from being struck by an oncoming train. It was the same Edison whose mother had to yank him out of school because he was too aggressive there with—questions; the same boy, the man, who would catch a couple of hours of sleep at night in his laboratory, while he pressed on and pressed on, testing hundreds of kinds of filaments until he found the right one—one that would persist in luminescence and would not require high voltage—for the electric light bulb.

Boys will not clear a bar set low. That is a paradox of their nature. They will not rise to the mediocre occasion. They fall below it. They do not need assistance and hand-holding. They need challenge and danger. That is the testimony of every human culture. Hannibal drives his elephants over the Alps, much to the astonishment of the natives. Alexander, advised that there was no way to conquer Tyre, because its fortress rested upon an island, and its walls came clear down to the sea, tried for months to lay siege to it, and he failed. But he then did what no one had conceived of doing before. He could not attack the city by sea. So he attacked it by land, by first *joining it to the land.* He made the island into a peninsula, building a causeway to it from the coast, and then letting his army pour in upon it.

Say to the boy, "Here is a plot of land covered with trees. I will give you the equipment to clear out the trees and the stumps. If you can do that, we will dig a swimming pool there." See what happens. The principle, you see, is that of the underlying power which in man can have a multitude of expressions. Without the desire to fight and to defeat the worthy foe, we do not have bridges, ships, towers, cities, pipes that bring fresh and clean water to our homes, and electric wires that bring the world to us at the click of a finger. All recommendations that boys should be tame and mild and inoffensive must break against the rocks of nature. The better thing to do is to train and direct the healthy desire to fight. A river that spills into and over a field does no good work. When it is channeled and its force is focused upon the mill wheel, it can grind out the corn; at a place like Hoover Dam, it can turn the mighty electromagnetic turbine to provide power for millions of people.

Conquest of the Self

In our time, the scapegoat for every social problem, it appears, is "toxic masculinity." That is what happens when people who are ill suited for abstract thought and who are not trained in history or even in man's difficult encounter with the natural world get hold of an idea, or less than an idea, a tag or slogan parading as an idea. There is no such thing as "toxic masculinity," no more than there is such a thing as "toxic femininity." There are good men and there are bad men. There are good women and there are bad women. Bad men will usually be bad as men are bad, and bad women will usually be bad as women are bad. And in my observation, outside of flagrant crimes that require extreme aggression and some considerable physical strength and risk, women are every bit as inventive as men when it comes to thinking of ways to make other people's lives miserable. We are all sinners.

We want boys to be more masculine, not less; we want them to be *gentlemen*. We want girls to be more feminine also, not less; but that is another book to write, and I am not its author. But boys cannot be really masculine unless they have engaged and fought and been victorious in the fundamental battle of the human soul. They must first conquer *themselves*.

It should be obvious that that is not going to be easy in a narcissistic age, when people define themselves by their feelings, especially their lusts, and when it is considered an act of hatred, even of downright violence, if you should dare to question Narcissus or Narcissa about what he or she sees in that shallow pool. But self-conquest is an absolute necessity for the gentleman. The clearest reason why is the most pragmatic. A boy will grow taller and stronger than his mother at around age thirteen or fourteen. *He must learn to restrain his strength.* He must learn never to raise a hand in anger against a woman, under any circumstances. He must learn that the first enemy to conquer is the unruliness of his own passions.

I have heard all my life long that boys should be encouraged to show their feelings, but they were mostly liars who said so. They never wanted me to show my real feelings. They are happy when boys weep, and when there is cause to weep, no man should look with scorn upon the boy who does so. They are content when boys say they are frightened. But if any boy should show the high-spirited feelings of disdain for what is mean and cowardly, or feelings of boyish anger against those who do wrong, or boyish contempt for mere softness and self-comforting, let alone boyish admiration for the hero, then all at once their care for feelings is nowhere to be found. Boys used to be taught to restrain the unruly and unhelpful passions and reject those that are unjust and foolish, and to nourish and direct those that are high-minded and generous and manly. Now it appears that they are taught to repress the manly and nourish mere weakness. Voluble lies have replaced honest silence.

The tragedy of Shakespeare's Romeo is that he is still a mere boy, whose parents in their long feud with the Capulets have unknowingly set a mine in the midst of Verona. The Montagues and the Capulets have not restrained *their* passions, much to the harm of the city, and so Romeo and Juliet do not learn to restrain theirs. Romeo falls out of love with his old flame Rosalind as soon as he sets eyes on Juliet, nor can his ghostly father, Friar Lawrence, persuade him to go more slowly. The tragedy of Othello is that the noble Moor who has conquered every enemy of the Venetian republic has not quite conquered his deep superstitions and his passionate jealousy. The near-tragedy of *The Tempest* comes about because the good duke Prospero would prefer to read books in his study than to govern Milan, and he gives in to that understandable desire, conceding all practical affairs to his brother Antonio—awaking an evil nature in him that ends in the subjugation of Milan to Naples, and the near death of Prospero and his baby girl Miranda. Lassitude no less than passion is a thing to be overcome, and so we find Prince Hal, who has spent his youth among wastrels and the amiable coward and ruffian Falstaff, determining to leave off his old ways and shine out all the more splendidly for having lived so long in the twilight.

Let boys know that their feelings are both very important and not important at all. The passions are good; they are the drive, the powerful horses that pull the chariot, but they must be trained, and when it comes to determining what is true, or what is the right thing to do, they are neither here nor there. Let boys know that if they would be true men, they must keep their promises *regardless of their feelings.* Let them know that in the pursuit of truth, what you desire *is of no consequence.* The bad man to fear is not usually the one who can set his feelings to the side. The bad man to fear is more usually the one who sets his passions upon the throne or arms them with a gun.

Odysseus, held captive on the island by the goddess Calypso, is never persuaded in his heart that he ought to remain there. It is the same Odysseus who would not allow his heart to be vitiated by the lotos, so that he would no longer pursue his long and hardship-ridden journey home, but would yield to feelings of futility, and the desire for peace. It is the same Odysseus who *does not* eat of the oxen of the sun god, no matter how hungry he is. Odysseus is no Victorian imperialist with a stiff upper lip. He is a man of intense and often violent passion, and that sometimes does get him into trouble, as when he dares to utter his name to the Cyclops Polyphemus, whom he has blinded. But even when he sees his son Telemachus for the first time, and his heart would go out to him, he hangs back, incognito, watching, speaking to the boy, testing him, waiting for just the right moment to reveal his identity.

I have been speaking here of boys and men in a natural sense, but the real conquest over the self can only be won by the grace of God—something that Homer did not know. I will then end this chapter with thoughts of my father, a man of deep and straightforward faith. When I was eighteen and a freshman at Princeton, my father suffered through a couple of months of regular physical exhaustion. He could hardly make it through the daytime without sleep. The doctor could find nothing wrong. Once, when he and my uncles were out hunting deer, he sat down in the snow against a tree and thought he would never get up from that place again. They finally sent him to a specialist, and it was discovered that very little blood was getting from his heart to the rest of his body. He could have died on that day in the woods. So they scheduled him for open heart surgery.

This was in 1978, when the operation was still rather rare, and surgeons who could perform it were few. My father never once gave us any sign that he was worried. The surgeon was a good man, he said, one of the first in that field, and one of the best. Everything would be all right. My father was such an able persuader, and so thorough was his mastery over fear—not that he was not afraid, because I think he was, but that he did not let fear seize the reins—that we hardly believed otherwise than that he would be in and out of the hospital in a couple of weeks, and that was all there was to it. When I visited him, shortly after the operation, I saw before me a physical wreck, a human being who had been brought to within an inch of death. It shocked me, such was the force of his conquest over fear, or his conquest over his natural desire to show his fear to us. He did not want us to fear, and so he kept his feelings to himself.

He had been a cigarette smoker and a beer drinker since he was a teenager, and now he must give up both of those pleasant habits, which he did, instantly, and without one complaint. He had to change his diet, and stop eating most of his favorite dishes, which he also did, instantly, and without complaint. For a year afterwards, he could walk only slowly, so that to be at his side was like watching over a man in his eighties and not his forties, but he did that too without complaint. The surgery was successful, but four years later, the doctors discovered cancerous polyps in my father's colon, and that began another period in his life, a nine-year fight against the cancer, to which he finally succumbed in 1991.

I remember him on the last day of his life. He was home, where he wanted to be. He could neither eat nor drink. His face was yellow with jaundice, the sign of a liver no longer doing its job. The priest, his good friend, had come to give him the viaticum. Some of my aunts and uncles and cousins stopped by, briefly, to say goodbye. He was awake through it all, and conscious, though his voice could not rise beyond a whisper.

I do not think that my father could ever have lived that final day as he lived it unless he had been a man of faith, and not because he himself was the source of the faith, but because the faith was given to him by God, along with its many and potent graces. He had never known any woman besides my mother. They had gone in purity to the altar. They had lived together for thirty-one years, and had loved one another wholly and devotedly, without sentimentality, but with clear and daily signs that they rejoiced in one another's company. Now it was to end, at least on this side of the grave. When the crisis came and his breath grew short and interrupted, I and my siblings huddled around him and touched him, while my mother leaned over him and he whispered his final words into her ear, "I love you." It was the death of a good Christian man—and I intend all three descriptors. He was good, he was Christian, and he was a man.

A boy like me, given as my father never was to sentiment and self-concern, could have had no better father to emulate.

Life to Give

And here we come to the end, or to the real beginning.

"When education is under direction of the Church, the entire man is educated," wrote Father Eligius Weir, after three years of speaking with and ministering to the hardened criminals in the Illinois State Penitentiary, and defending them against charge that they were born to be criminals, or that they were mere scum, unlike the upper class embezzlers, bribe takers, and swindlers who were very occasionally caught and imprisoned to swell their numbers. "The physical, intellectual, and moral part of man is trained," he continued. "To neglect the training of any part of man is to develop a monstrosity. To form the mind to follow correct moral principles but to omit to train the will is only sharpening the tools of a crook." Read that sentence over again. To the extent that we form the mind at all, we train it to follow false moral principles or none. Evil is the result. Boys, stronger than their sisters and more attracted to danger, will thus rack up plenty of crimes, and of the countable sort, though their sisters will be female monstrosities as well, doing what they can in subtler ways to make the world a darker place, and happy to do so.

But we have the ultimate call, the ultimate aim, toward which to direct the soul of the boy. "Greater love than this no man has," says Jesus, "than to lay down his life for his friends."

Women give life from their very bodies, every time they give birth. Women give sustenance from their very substance. Do not cross the mother bear with her cubs. The sinister tiger Shere Khan, in Kipling's *The Jungle Book*, would sooner face Father Wolf than Mother Wolf, as he glares into the narrow opening of the wolves' den. She was called "Demon" when she was young, and her eyes bear out the wisdom of Kipling's poem, which informs us that despite all of the structures of government and law that men may devise, "the female of the species is more deadly than the male." The female will fight to the death for her own, and she knows no foreign policy that would subordinate the welfare of her own to the common weal. This is well and good, and only to be expected.

But what of the boy, and the boy who would become a man?

The Life of Life

I turn here to a scene from a fine novel by John Buchan, who wrote smart adventure stories that boys once read by the millions. The novel is *Sick Heart River*, set in the forbidding northlands of Canada, in the valley of the Mackenzie River, which flows from its mountain sources in the south, twenty-four hundred miles north, to end in its swampy and usually frozen delta upon the Arctic Ocean. The story is set up by an appeal. A young Canadian American, Francois Galliard, has left his wife and his business in New York City—a business with international implications, just at the time that war is about to break out again in Europe. He has, it is thought, gone off on a mystical search for his roots, exploring the wastes of the Canadian shield, and so some friends of his come to a British adventurer whom they trust, one Edward Leithen, to seek him out—in a vast territory, almost a million square miles and nearly uninhabited—and bring him back home.

It turns out that Galliard has fallen in with another man with a mystical pull, a half-breed named Lew Frizel, who is searching for a kind of Shangri-La near the headwaters of the Mackenzie. For he had long ago seen a river there, the Sick Heart River, flowing amidst a sheltered valley, whose mountain walls had lent the place a warmth most unusual for the nearby lands. It was a place of rich green vegetation, flanked by the mountains and the fir forests and tundra beyond. Surely a man might live here and be free from the corruption of the world around! Hence the name of the river: it is for those who are sick of heart. Lew has "infected" Galliard with his passion, and they set out to find that river. Leithen sets out after them.

But there are complications. The first is that Edward Leithen is dying of tuberculosis. He had accepted the charge to go and find Galliard because he did not want to die idle in a room somewhere, but on his feet, like the fighter he had always been. The second is that the Sick Heart River is an illusion. Not that it does not exist, or that the greenery is not there. It does exist, and it is green. But there is no animal life. It is a river to break your heart, not heal it. The third is that Lew and Galliard have fallen out, each afflicted with a kind of madness, with Lew even abandoning Galliard to what ought to have been a certain death of exposure. The fourth is that while Leithen and a couple of Indians have found Lew and Galliard both and have managed to bring them back to sanity, a terrible despair has fallen upon the camp of the Indians at the Catholic mission, their headquarters; famine is in the land, and the Hare hunters seem determined to die of it, having lost all of the fight within them.

Leithen has nearly died in the journey, but it appears that the cold dry air is beginning to do his lungs some good, so that he might actually survive and live to a good old age. That is, if he does not tax his strength any farther, but here he must make his final decision. Lew and Galliard are saved, but the Hares will die, unless someone takes that whole situation in hand, and Leithen is the only man who can do it. His friends urge him against it, because they know that the strain will kill him. But Leithen knows what he must do:

> There was a plain task before him, to fight with Death. God for His own purpose had unloosed it in the world, ravening over places which had once been rich in innocent life. Here in the North life had always been on sufferance, its pale slender shoots fighting a hard battle against the Elder Ice. But it had maintained its brave defiance. And now one such pathetic slip was on the verge of extinction. This handful of Hares had for generations been a little enclave of life besieged by mortality. Now it was perishing, hurrying to share in the dissolution which was overtaking the world.
>
> By God's help that should not happen—the God who was the God of the living. Through strange circuits he had come to that simple forthright duty for which he had always longed. In that duty he must make his soul.

"This is a war and I obey orders," says Leithen. "I've got my orders. In a world where Death is king we're going to defy him and save life."

The Catholic missionary Father Duplessis, hearing these words, quotes in Latin the psalm: "There is a river, the streams whereof shall make glad the city of God." Leithen does in fact save the Hares from their own desire to die. He wears himself out in the task. When Easter approaches, he can barely speak, but he is calm and happy, and he attends Mass for the last time. He "would sit in a corner following my Latin with his lips," writes Duplessis, "and he seemed to draw comfort from it. I think the reason was that he was now sharing something with the Hares, and was not a director, but one of the directed. For he had come to love those poor childish folk. Hitherto a lonely man, he had found a clan and a family."

That would seem to be a far journey from the life of a mere boy. For boys, like their sisters, or even more than their sisters, do not have any opinion of time and its passage. Says King Polixenes in Shakespeare's *The Winter's Tale*, when his boyhood friend's wife asks him what they were like when they were children:

> *We were, fair queen,*
> *Two lads that thought there was no more behind,*
> *But such a day tomorrow as today,*
> *And to be boy eternal.*

We may think of John Greenleaf Whittier's glorious tribute to the free ways of a good and healthy boy:

> *Blessings on thee, little man,*
> *Barefoot boy, with cheek of tan!*
> *With thy turned-up pantaloons,*
> *And thy merry whistled tunes;*
> *With thy red lip, redder still*
> *Kissed by strawberries on the hill;*
> *With the sunshine on thy face,*
> *Through thy torn brim's jaunty grace;*
> *From my heart I give thee joy,—*
> *I was once a barefoot boy!*
> *Prince thou art,—the grown-up man*
> *Only is republican.*

Or we turn from that "little man," with all his boyishly serious and madcap purposes, to the essential boy, Peter Pan, a byword in our time for young men who will not grow up. Yet Peter himself, stranded with Wendy on a rock in the middle of the ocean with the tide rising high, ties the tail of a kite around her so that she will sail off in safety. "And you a lady; never," he says when she suggests that they draw lots to see who will be saved, and before she knows it, she is borne from his sight. Even Peter Pan knows what the right thing to do is, and why, and he takes up a pose before Death that is manly and boyish at once: "Peter was not quite like other boys; but he was afraid at last. A tremour ran through him, like a shudder passing over the sea; but on the sea one shudder follows another till there are hundreds of them, and Peter felt just the one. Next moment he was standing erect on the rock again, with that smile on his face and a drum beating within him. It was saying, 'To die will be an awfully big adventure.'"

Jesus says that he who wishes to save his life must lose it, and I have long thought that that was not a condition placed upon us by God from without, but an inner law of being itself. To be, to be a person in the full sense of the word, is to give yourself away to another: we do not lose ourselves by the gift, but find ourselves, or come to be ourselves in the first place. So there is an inner harmony between the boy's longing for adventure and the man's willingness to do what Leithen does in Buchan's story; it is not to seek thrills for their own sake, but to seek and to give love. In the end, it is to be alive by giving your life away.

Now think of how often boys "die" in their games. The cowboy shoots the Indian or the Indian shoots the cowboy. The cop shoots the robbers. The offensive guard, whose name nobody knows because he never catches the ball or carries it, gives up his body on every play to block for the running back or to protect the quarterback. The baseball player puts himself on the line for his team, in a game in which even the best hitters fail more often than they succeed. The basketball player on defense stands his ground and takes a ferocious offensive foul, for his team, that sends him sprawling to the floor. And any of these boys would readily understand why the fireman climbs up the side of a house ready to fall into matchsticks to save the life of an old man in a bedroom upstairs, or even, at the pleading of small children, to save the family dog.

When women say to boys, "We don't need you to do those physically strenuous things for us anymore," besides its being quite false, it cuts their hearts right out. It is as if to say, "You are useless." Boys need to be needed more than they need to be loved, or they need to be loved by being needed. It is indispensable to them that they should be *dispensable*, that is, needed to be spent up, for the women they love and the land they would protect, and, in the end, the faith they would affirm.

Suffer the Little Children

"I am the good shepherd," says Jesus. "I know my own and my own know me, as the Father knows me and I know the Father; and I lay down my life for the sheep." Why would the Father want the Son to do such a thing? Because it is the heart of life to do so. "For this reason the Father loves me," says Jesus, "because I lay down my life, that I may take it again. No one takes it from me, but I lay it down of my own accord" (Jn 10:14–15, 17–18). It is the same Jesus whom we see portrayed in many a painting, telling the disciples to cease playing the role of managers and defenders of the Master's rest, but to "let the children come to me, and do not hinder them; for to such belongs the kingdom of God" (Lk 18:16). In the scene painted by Hans Rottenhammer (1607), a perfect chaos of portly mothers and little toddling boys, the chief among them as naked as the day he was born, presses upon Jesus, who calmly welcomes them and blesses them and seems completely unaware of the troubled looks of his disciples, who are shaded into the background. That little boy cannot know that when he comes to Jesus, he comes to the man who says that the cost of discipleship is to take up the cross, and to follow the Master.

He cannot know it, but it would strike a sympathetic chord in his boyish nature. The old painters were fond of picturing Jesus as a boy carpenter, fashioning a cross, and though there never would have been a call for such an item of furniture, the sense of it is right, and is more joyful in its solemnity than are modern depictions of the boy Jesus doing appallingly sweet things and grinning like a trim and prim hero from a Horatio Alger success story. The boy is the father to the man, said Wordsworth, and so there is in the boy the stirrings of that same spirit that would rejoice in the gift of life, flung bravely away and therefore gained forever.

Is that not also the call that the boy hears for love in this world? "Husbands, love your wives," says Saint Paul, "as Christ loved the church and gave himself up for her" (Eph 5:25), and the good Christian man takes it not as a command so much as a confirmation and encouragement, because he is glad and proud to do so. Each sex is made for self-sacrifice, and this is the ideal form that it takes for boys and men in the context of human love, the love of a man for a woman. Says Adam to Eve, on that fateful morning imagined by Milton, when much to his purpose Satan would find the married couple apart from one another:

> *The wife, where danger or dishonor lurks,*
> *Safest and seemliest by her husband stays,*
> *Who guards her, or with her the worst endures.*

If this wisdom strikes any of us now as quaint or even offensive, I should like to ask what great success in married love and the establishment of strong families our wise society can claim? Let boys learn that their boyishness is not for the abuse of women, or for their crass domination, but for giving, giving to the point of danger and even, in the ultimate case, death. And let girls learn to accept the gift with grace, because there is a grace in gratitude as well as in giving, and many will be the time when the boy or the man must blush and receive a gift from her. No life but in gifts.

So if we would put Jesus' words into the masculine gender and say, "Let the boys come to me, and hinder them not, for of such"—and we might imagine a really scampish corner of it, with eternal blessings as are fit for a Huck Finn—"is the kingdom of heaven," we might see Jesus as loving not some abstract ideal of childhood but the real flesh-and-blood creatures before him, the children, and they come in two sexes and only two, boys and girls. We might then come closer to making the connection between natural boyhood and supernatural Christian manhood, and it would be as if that raffish boy named Benjamin had tied an iron key to a kite during an electric storm, and welcomed the lightning.

The Boy as Saint

A tall and strikingly handsome young man stands, his arms folded, atop an alpine peak, with a pipe hanging jauntily from the side of his mouth. He is wearing a striped shirt, his head is bare, and his alpenstock is planted firmly in the ice beside him. He is Pier Giorgio Frassati (1901–1925), beatified by Pope John Paul II in 1990.

The life of Pier Giorgio may serve as a model of boyhood, not just for its sanctity, but for its sanctity in boyish form. He was a remarkably intelligent lad who did not do well in school. Have we not met many such? When he failed his exams at age twelve, his father, the wealthy and agnostic owner of a liberal newspaper, sent him to a school run by Jesuits, where the boy acquired a reputation among his peers for his intelligence, regardless of what his grades might have been; the boy was adept in German, French, and Latin, along with his native Italian.

He was a boy of spirit, what Plato called *thymos,* that drive that C. S. Lewis, following Plato's lead, associated with neither the brain nor the belly but the chest. Here is Pier Giorgio addressing a gathering of Catholic youth and speaking about the Holy Eucharist: "When you are totally consumed by the Eucharistic fire, then you will be able more consciously to thank God, who has called you to become part of His family. Then you will enjoy the peace that those who are happy in this world have never experienced, because true happiness, oh young people, does not consist in the pleasures of this world, or in earthly things, but in peace of conscience, which we only have if we are pure of heart and mind."

Fire, fire! The one time when it is good to cry fire in a crowded room: when you are giving your heart to others, and encouraging them to light the fire of Eucharistic ardor within. These are not the words of a prissy young man who would not deign to get his fingers dirty in the mire of life. Pier Giorgio was a man of action: indeed of Catholic Action, the group that he took part in, and the Saint Vincent de Paul Society, and the Dominican Order, whereof he was a lay member. He gave to the poor constantly, from the time he was a boy.

"Every day that passes," he said, "I fall more desperately in love with the mountains." That feeling is in harmony with the Psalmist, who cried, "I lift up my eyes to the hills," whence his help should come (Ps 121:1). The young Frassati said that life was good in so far as we live it "al di là," the fine Italian phrase meaning "over in the world beyond," and that made his life here in the world not less exciting but more, always more. He hated Fascism and set his jaw like flint against it. In thinking of the Beatitude, "Blessed are you when men revile you and persecute you and utter all kinds of evil against you falsely on my account" (Mt 5:11), Frassati had this to say: "The times we live in are hard, because the persecution against the Church is growing more fierce and cruel than ever, but you young people, good and bold as you are, you must not be afraid of this little period, but you must hold present in your mind the fact that the Church is a divine institution that will never come to an end" (my translation).

With twelve young men like Pier Giorgio Frassati, you might conquer the world. But he was not long for this one. He was boating on the Po River with some friends when he was stricken with poliomyelitis, and he died a few days later, at the age of twenty-four.

Or we might look to the pattern of Saint Dominic Savio (1842–1857), a boy who entered the school founded by Saint John Bosco in Turin, and whose biography was written by his saintly teacher after his death. Unlike Pier Giorgio, Dominic Savio was of slight build and a frail constitution. He was handsome in a delicate way. Also unlike Pier Giorgio, he was always the most studious of boys, learning every lesson quickly and easily. But he had the same boyish spirit of launching forth into adventure, and the same contempt for safety. "Death, rather than sin," was one of his mottos.

As for the prospect of death, John Bosco wrote that "he had no misgivings about this himself, and had often said: 'I must hurry, or else night will overtake me on the way,' which meant that he had only a short time left to him, and that he should use it well in the performance of good works. It is the custom at the Oratory for the boys," the teacher went on to say, "to make the exercises for a good death every month. This consists chiefly in approaching the Sacraments of Confession and Holy Communion as though it were to be for the last time. Pius IX had granted several indulgences to this pious exercise. Dominic always made this preparation for a good death with an exactitude that could not be excelled. Among the prayers said in public on this day are an Our Father and a Hail Mary for the one amongst us who shall be the first to die. On one of the monthly exercise days, Dominic playfully said, 'Instead of saying "for the first one amongst us who is to die," it ought rather to be: "for Dominic Savio, who will be the first one amongst us to die."' And this he remarked on more than one occasion."

Dominic would not be the sort to get into a scrap, but he had the boy's relish for combat nonetheless, and for the friendship that would make him stronger, as steel sharpens steel. So it is that he became friends with another boy studying to become a priest, named John Massiglia. John Bosco very much approved of their friendship, and notes this moment in their conversation after the Easter Communion: "I very much desire that we should be true friends," said Dominic to John, "friends, that is, in regard to the affairs of the soul. I propose that from now we each admonish the other in regard to anything that may be thought useful for our spiritual advancement. If you see anything wrong in my conduct tell me immediately, that I may correct it; or if you think of any good I ought to perform, point it out to me."

Does the reader recall Tom Sawyer's band of robbers and their blood oaths in the cave by the Mississippi? Here is Dominic Savio doing the same kind of thing, after Pope Pius IX had declared the dogma of the Immaculate Conception:

> Young Savio was always practical in his manifestation of fervour. His idea was not only to celebrate the event, but to set on foot something that might be a permanent remembrance, and might be productive in years to come of a continual stream of devout clients of Our Lady.
>
> He therefore set to work amongst his closest friends, and proposed to them the formation of a sodality or association, to be called the Sodality of the Immaculate Conception. Its object was to obtain the special protection of Our Lady during life and particularly at the hour of

death. The means proposed were to practice and promote acts of devotion in honour of the Mother of God, and the adoption of the practice of frequent Communion by all members. It was to have a special rule and these were the subject of long consideration, so that they were only in their final shape by June 8th, 1856, about nine months before his death. These were read out by him before the Altar of Our Lady on that day. The articles were of an exhaustive character, twenty-one in number, providing for the regular meeting of the members, the spiritual duties undertaken, and the means for gaining the chief ends mentioned above. These rules were all submitted to the judgment of the Director, and concluded with an appeal to Our Blessed Lady to assist the associates and bless their efforts.

Give boys the opportunity to join a pious league led by girls and filled with the spirit of girlish enthusiasm, and they will decline, not out of bigotry, but simply because it will fail to catch their interest. Give them the opportunity to form their own leagues, as boys have always done, everywhere and in every age, and see what happens. Let them become the fighting saints they are meant to be.

Behold, I Make All Things New

I will end with a Christian consideration. The Greeks idolized youth, and that was a sad kind of thing, because time will do its work, and youth must give way to age. The Romans honored age, and there was always something old about them, hard and practical and prey to cold cynicism. They built earthly things they thought would last forever, but no earthly thing does. All fall prey to time and change. Horace might say that in his poetry he had built for himself a monument more enduring than bronze, but he was also the pleasantly sad fellow who told us that we should seize the day, because no one knows what will come with the morrow.

Yet Jesus says that unless we become as little children, we shall not enter the kingdom of heaven, and Saint John addresses his letters to his followers, whom he affectionately calls "little children," and the same saint saw the One seated upon the throne in his vision of the consummation of the world, who says, "Behold, I make all things new" (Rv 21:5). In Fra Angelico's painting of the Final Judgment, we see youthful saints, male and female, looking upon the triumphant Christ and greeting one another, while off to the side, in a garden decked with flowers, are dancing small boys and girls, hand in hand with angels. Milton's angels are youthful, and the most attractive among them, Ithuriel and Zephon, who catch Satan in the form of a toad whispering evil suggestions into the ear of the sleeping Eve, are "stripling cherubs," "severe in youthful beauty."

The Christian faith does not make a fetish of youth, nor does it do homage to age for age's sake. "We shall all be changed," says Saint Paul of the resurrection, "in a moment, in the twinkling of an eye" (1 Cor 15:51–52). Perhaps that is why Caravaggio, in his *Supper at Emmaus*, portrays the risen Jesus as a beardless young man, too young to be recognized by the disciples, until he broke the bread at table with them and so manifested himself. Mary, says Georges Bernanos, is "younger than sin," not older. Then we may wonder what kind of frolic youthfulness, in male and female form, in boyish hallooing and girlish grace, will be found among the saints in heaven. Our God too is younger than we are, the Ancient of Days who is ever new.

So I imagine a man's first glimpse of heaven may be like so:

What shall we see first, in the reign of God?
Our vision cannot comfortably behold

Towers of emerald-stone and thrones of gold
And glassy oceans flowing free and broad.
Perhaps when we awake
And rub the film of greatness from our eyes,
We'll see a small boy sitting at a lake,
Guiding his fishing-pole by gentle thumb,
Who turns to us without the least surprise
To say, "At last—I thought you'd never come."

Dear Reader, may it be so for you and yours.